gestalten

The MONOCLE
Travel Guide Series

Copenhagen

For more information,
please visit *gestalten.com*

———

Bibliographic information
published by the Deutsche
Nationalbibliothek: The Deutsche
Nationalbibliothek lists this publication in the Deutsche National-
bibliografie; detailed bibliographic
data are available online
at *dnb.d-nb.de*

This book was printed on
paper certified by the FSC®

Monocle editor in chief:
Tyler Brûlé
Monocle editor: *Andrew Tuck*
Books editor: *Joe Pickard*
Guide editor: *Amy Richardson*

———

Designed by *Monocle*
Proofreading by *Monocle*
Typeset in *Plantin & Helvetica*

———

Printed by *Offsetdruckerei
Grammlich, Pliezhausen*

Made in Germany

Published by *Gestalten*, Berlin 2016
ISBN 978-3-89955-682-7

© Die Gestalten Verlag GmbH &
Co. KG, Berlin 2016

Welcome
—— Model city

Wonderful, wonderful Copenhagen. There are plenty of reasons why the Danish capital regularly tops MONOCLE's Quality of Life survey – quite simply, it's a glorious place to both live and visit. The compact, *environmentally conscious* city of 1.2 million people has a bountiful urban environment: miles of *harbourfront promenades*, lush parks, a striking blend of *contemporary and historic architecture* and public spaces that invite passersby to stop for a few moments and soak it all up.

Sure, the winters may be long but with so many *hyggeligt cafés*, bars and restaurants, plus a dynamic selection of retailers, who minds spending a little time indoors? This is, after all, the birthplace of *New Nordic cuisine* and *Danish Modern design*, and the quality of the food, drink and shopping today upholds these weighty legacies.

MONOCLE's team of editors and reporters have ventured far and wide to collate their favourite elements of the city. Look past the bright lights of *Tivoli Gardens* to see how *clever urban planning* left its mark in the form of user-friendly transport infrastructure and spaces for people to relax and socialise in. We'll introduce you to the gallerists and independent shop owners making sure that Copenhagen retains its reputation as a *creative hotspot*. You'll also find recommendations for where to rest your head, the best late-night cocktail bars and a few scenic running routes to work off all that *smørrebrød*.

Copenhagen is a model for what can happen when a city puts people first. Come and see for yourself. — (M)

Contents
—— Navigating the city

Use the key below to explore the guide section by section.

 Hotels

 Food and drink

 Retail

 Things we'd buy

E Essays

C Culture

D Design and architecture

S Sport and fitness

W Walks

Map
—— A city shaped by water

A closer inspection of Copenhagen's topography reveals a peculiar picture. Water cuts distinctive forms: there's the star-shaped Kastellet fortress, the 3km-long skinny stretch of lakes and the crescent-moon canal that cups Christianshavn. Many of these weaving waterways were created at the behest of military-savvy town planners and a king dazzled by the whimsy of Venice.

These bodies of water help to demarcate the neighbourhoods that splay from the city centre in finger-like fashion. Southwest of the harbour you'll find the vibrant Meatpacking District; while the steadily regenerating expanse of Amager and pretty Christianshavn (now more easily accessible thanks to a new footbridge linking the neighbourhood with Nyhavn) are east of it; to the west of the lakes is Frederiksberg and fashionable Nørrebro. So for a glimpse into the city's rich history and a hint of its future direction, we recommend navigating its waterways.

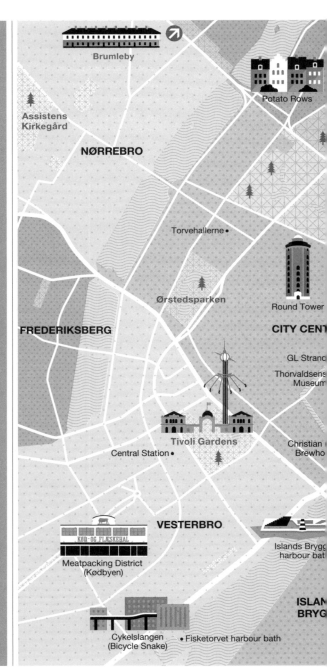

Brumleby

Assistens Kirkegård

NØRREBRO

Potato Rows

Torvehallerne •

Ørstedsparken

Round Tower

FREDERIKSBERG

CITY CENT

GL Strand

Thorvaldsens Museum

Tivoli Gardens

Central Station •

Christian Brewho

VESTERBRO

KØD-OG FLÆSKEHAL

Meatpacking District (Kødbyen)

Islands Brygg harbour bat

Cykelslangen (Bicycle Snake)

• Fisketorvet harbour bath

ISLAN BRYG

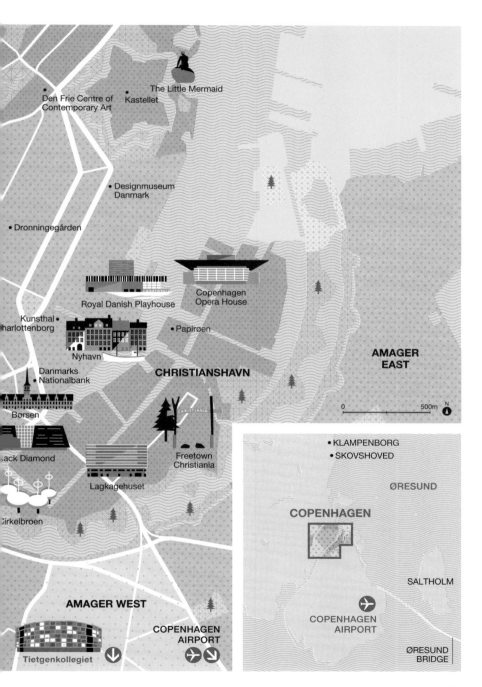

The Little Mermaid

Den Frie Centre of
Contemporary Art
Kastellet

Designmuseum
Danmark

Dronningegården

Royal Danish Playhouse

Copenhagen
Opera House

Kunsthal
Charlottenborg

Papirøen

Nyhavn

Danmarks
Nationalbank

CHRISTIANSHAVN

AMAGER
EAST

Børsen

CHRISTIANIA

0   500m   N

Black Diamond

Freetown
Christiania

Lagkagehuset

Cirkelbroen

KLAMPENBORG
SKOVSHOVED

ØRESUND

COPENHAGEN

SALTHOLM

AMAGER WEST

COPENHAGEN
AIRPORT

COPENHAGEN
AIRPORT

Tietgenkollegiet

ØRESUND
BRIDGE

Need to
know
—— Get to grips
with the basics

Copenhageners are generally a friendly and accepting crowd – what else would you expect in a country that has a special word for sharing good times with others? But that's not to say you can't smooth the way for yourself too – here are some insider tips for visitors to the city, from getting around to learning the lingo.

Tongue twisters
The language

The Danish language is notoriously difficult to speak and some (particularly in other Scandinavian countries) claim that it's becoming increasingly difficult to understand too. Aside from the standard 26-letter alphabet the Danes have three additional letters – Æ, Ø, Å – plus a sprinkling of glottal stops. What's more, the Danes only pronounce certain sections of every word, so written and spoken Danish are very different beasts. How do you know when you've cracked the language? When you can pronounce the 51-letter *Speciallaegepraksisplanlaeg-ningsstabiliseringsperiode*. It means something about planning periods for medical specialists. Never mind...

In all their majesty
The royal family

The Danes love their royals and with good reason – there are few monarchs as deserving of kudos as head matriarch Queen Margrethe II. Her achievements stretch beyond having three degrees and five languages; she also makes her own clothes (her costume designs have been worn on stage by members of the Royal Danish Ballet) and is an accomplished artist whose exhibitions regularly tour the country. And another – ahem – crowning achievement? She helped translate *The Lord of the Rings* into Danish. The Danes are also very proud of how down-to-earth their royals are – Crown Princess Mary can often be seen cycling her twins to school on a Christiania bike.

Feeling good
Hygge

There's one uniquely Danish term you're guaranteed to hear during your stay: *hygge* (pronounced hu-gar). No, it's not a verb for a Dane getting up close and cuddly (although that too can be involved); the word most often used by way of explanation is "cosy". But it's not all about candles and a comfy sofa: a *hyggeligt* moment could be enjoying a beer on a warm day in a park (or even a cemetery, *see page 139*). Basically it's all about the good vibes.

Hyggeligt vibes? That's the spirit

The ride stuff
Cycling

As you'd expect in the hometown of lauded urbanist Jan Gehl (*see page 102*), Copenhagen is a cyclist's paradise and if you're going to spend time here, you simply must saddle up. We've outlined all you need to know, from the road rules (*see page 124*) and routes (*see page 126*) to a rundown on cycling culture (*see page 071*). A tip: hire a ride from a bike shop rather than sticking out like a tourist on a clunky (though admittedly user-friendly) Bycyklen bike.

Well that's one way to get some time away from the nest

Smiles better
Quality of life

If you've heard the Danes are the happiest people on Earth you may be disappointed to find not everyone is a well-dressed hipster larking about on a bike; middle-aged women flipping their middle fingers in fits of road rage are quite common too. Many experts believe this reputation for happiness is down to the equality of Danish society: there is not a huge difference between the living standards of the most wealthy and the least. (For an excellent exploration of the subject see MONOCLE writer Michael Booth's book *The Almost Nearly Perfect People*.) Another quirk of the culture is the high level of public trust – mothers often leave babies in prams outside on the street while they shop.

Polite society
Danish manners

While it's true that there is technically no word for "please" and the Danes pride themselves on their informal, egalitarian society, that doesn't mean there aren't etiquette protocols. When greeting a group of Danes, shake hands with all parties

(even children), starting with the women.

Punctuality is paramount and always bring a small gift if invited to a Danish home for a meal (wrapped flowers or chocolates will suffice; don't be surprised when these are opened upon receipt). And always wait until your host toasts the meal with a "*Skål*" before tucking in. (All that said, swear words are employed enthusiastically by everyone from young kids and senior citizens to newspaper headlines. There's no Danish equivalent so English profanities have been appropriated and are thrown about with reckless abandon.)

Revenue raisers
Tax

Copenhagen has first-rate healthcare, education for all, low poverty, clean streets, renewable energy, excellent public infrastructure... and it all costs. A 42 to 62 per cent hit to each week's pay to be exact, and that's just income tax – there's a host of others, such as 25 per cent on all purchases. In most other countries people would be reaching for picket signs but the majority of Danes think it's worth it; the Danish word for tax – *skat* – also means "treasure" or "darling".

Tax accounting is certainly thirsty work in Copenhagen

Time to head out
Eating and drinking

Many visitors are caught out by early dining times in Copenhagen; peak reservation time is 18.30 to 19.30 and people are usually wobbling home on their bicycles by 21.00 or 22.00. However, some of the more modern places are now seating people later than 21.00. While the food scene is compact the quality is extremely high – with prices to match – and as such going out for a meal is considered a treat for most people.

Recipes for success
New Nordic

It's impossible to eat or drink in the capital and not acknowledge the legacy of Noma. When Claus Meyer returned to Copenhagen after years abroad studying cultural connections to food, he teamed up with René Redzepi to open Noma and create the New Nordic Food Manifesto, advocating seasonality, sustainability, purity and quality. Many of the top tables in town are run by Noma alumni, and the New Nordic ethos is one of the country's most popular exports.

A little something extra
Tipping

Whether in restaurants, taxis or hotels, prices tend to include service and all taxes. Hospitality staff earn decent pay so there's no need to tip but if you would like to, 10 per cent of the bill is fine. Cards can be used almost everywhere and splitting bills won't raise any eyebrows.

Hotels
—— Homes away from home

Communal hub
——
The bar is a popular spot for after-work drinks

Surprisingly for a city with such a strong design heritage, the hotel offering in Copenhagen has traditionally been a tad poor. A focus on appealing to the conference crowd has led to a slew of hotels with 100-plus rooms but there is still a paucity of elegantly kitted-out independents.

You'll find our pick of the crop over the following pages, plus a slick set of self-catering apartments and some luxury options in the form of storied Hotel d'Angleterre and the Radisson Blu Royal Hotel, the passion project of designer Arne Jacobsen.

Happily, most operators do capitalise on the Danish cultural phenomenon of *hygge*; cosy communal spaces are considered vital and guests are encouraged to make themselves at home in them. Often this takes the form of a convivial sundowner each day and the invitation is extended to the wider community, making Copenhagen's hotel bars some of the liveliest places to become 17.00.

①
Hotel SP34, City Centre
Contemporary cool

Hotel SP34's urbane bent is testimony to the design-minded approach deployed by family-run Brøchner Hotels. One of the group's former posts in the Latin Quarter and its neighbouring apartment building were gutted and rebuilt in 2014 to form this 118-room hotel complete with terrace bar, gym, conference centre and mini cinema.

Danish architect and designer Morten Hedegaard led the renovations and owners Søren and Mette Brøchner-Mortensen assisted with interiors; the result is an effortlessly cool ensemble of contemporary rooms. The lobby bar is attended by helpful staff who will pour your daily complimentary glass of wine at 17.00. And Väkst, one of three in-house restaurants, is run by the talented team behind Höst.
34 Sankt Peders Straede, 1453
+45 3313 3000
brochner-hotels.dk

MONOCLE COMMENT: Like any good Danish design hotel, there's furniture from revered names such as Frits Henningsen but also some surprises. During renovations the team found a 1950s chair of unknown origin and put it back in production. It's now a SP34 signature and can be found in guest rooms.

Must dash – my complimentary glass of wine won't drink itself

② Stay Copenhagen, Islands Brygge
Corporate luxe

The foyer of these 172 serviced apartments feels like the offices of a smart start-up but the building has a rich history. Built as a workingman's hotel, the A-House became a home to artists such as Tal R in the early 2000s, at which point Stay was on the drawing board. Its A-shaped floor plan is the same but everything else was gutted for the apartments, which opened in 2010.

Options range from studios to three-bedders. There's parking too but the location in one of the newer harbourside zones cries out for bike-riding. Take the Cykelslangen across to the Meatpacking District or pedal to Islands Brygge park for a swim.
79A Islands Brygge, 2300
+45 7244 4434
staycopenhagen.dk

MONOCLE COMMENT: Stay in the Copenhagen Loft XL, a 150 sq m space with exposed concrete beams and ceilings that reveals the building's former life

③

Babette Guldsmeden, City Centre
Danish design meets Indonesia

The Guldsmeden group operates
no fewer than four hotels in the city,
but Babette is the most refined of the
bunch, not least because it's the only
one not based in lively (but still a tad
scruffy) Vesterbro. Instead, Babette
is directly opposite the star-shaped
Kastellet fortress in the city's elegant
art and antiques district.

The 98-room hotel was renovated
in 2013 to add balconies to its
south-facing façade, a rare feature
for hotels in Copenhagen. And while
the mix of Danish and Indonesian
furniture and homeware doesn't
sound great on paper, in reality it
works: rooms are small but bright
and tactile touches such as sheepskin
throws, curtains on the four-poster
beds and plenty of colourful
cushions and lively art create a
warm, slightly bohemian effect.

On the roof there's a Balinese-
inspired spa and sauna (complete
with a wooden bucket shower
for cooling off) which has some
of the best views in the city. The
restaurant serves food all day (the
majority of which is organic) and
the bar is often buzzing thanks
to its popularity among the
neighbourhood's fashionable set.
78 Bredgade, 1260
+45 3314 1500
guldsmedenhotels.com

Eco credentials
90 per cent
of the food
and drink is
organic

*It's no
birdbath but
I'm quite
partial to the
rooftop bucket
shower*

④ Ibsens Hotel, Nansensgade
Style and grace

The Nansensgade neighbourhood is lined with elegant old buildings and is home to vintage-furniture shops, art galleries and boutiques – with not a chain outlet in sight. The Brøchner family of the Arthur Group, owners of Ibsens, drew on this independent, eclectic atmosphere when it revamped the hotel in 2011.

The lobby feels like a hip Copenhagener's living room and is filled with pieces from local artists, makers and vendors. The wooden dining tables were crafted by 100-year-old cabinet-makers Jul. Møller & Søns and the industrial French lamps were discovered at antique shop No.40. It makes for an intimate space where guests are encouraged to mingle over a drink during "cosy hour" (from 17.00).

The 118 rooms come in six varieties (from Junior Suite to X-Large).
23 Vendersgade, 1363
+45 3345 7744
arthurhotels.dk/ibsens-hotel/

MONOCLE COMMENT: While it doesn't have its own restaurant, the Arthur Group owns the block and has leased various spaces to restaurants and cafés. Guests can charge meals back to their room.

Shine a light
⎯
Nimb Hotel
is lined with
coloured light
bulbs

5
Nimb Hotel, Vesterbro
Secret garden party

Its sleek black façade on
Bernstorffsgade may not give
much away but walk onto the
back terrace and the hotel's
extravagant structure is revealed.
A Moorish-style palace covered in
1,000 coloured lightbulbs, Nimb
faces straight onto Tivoli Gardens
amusement park and guests
are treated to daily tickets for
its rides. All 17 rooms but one have
views over the atmospheric grounds
and no two are the same; they were
designed by René Jasper Thomsen to
mix antique and modern furniture.

From underground Vinothek
restaurant to the smørrebrod
parlour Fru Nimb, dishes at the
hotel's five restaurants range
from French delicacies to Scandi
classics. Breakfast is served at
Nimb Brasserie with eggs laid by
chickens reared inside the gardens,
and afternoon tea in the former
ballroom comes arranged in no
less than the shape of Tivoli's
fanciful architecture.

Open the windows on summery
Friday evenings to hear gigs taking
place on Tivoli's stage; but if you're
at ground floor, be sure to keep out
the peacocks.
5 Bernstorffsgade, 1577
+45 8870 0000
nimb.dk

(6)
Avenue Hotel Copenhagen,
Frederiksberg
Home comforts

SP34 (*see page 16*) may be the
city's slickest designer hotel but
its Brøchner Hotels stablemate is
among the most comfy. The lounge
area of the gracious building is
a study in *hygge*, with brimming
bookshelves and chocolate-brown
velvet sofas that beg to be sat on.

Built in 1898 by Emil Blichfeldt,
who created Tivoli Gardens'
landmark entrance, the former
residential building was converted
into a hotel in 1939. Its 68 rooms are
simple but homely, complemented
by Missoni bedspreads.

The courtyard is a lovely place
to sprawl during the hotel's "wine
hour" from 17.00. You're likely
to be rubbing shoulders with
Copenhageners who live nearby.
"We offer residents in the area a
membership card so that they can
use our facilities," says CEO Karim
Nielsen. "This creates a nice, local
feeling for our guests."
29 Åboulevard, 1960
+45 3537 3111
avenuehotel.dk

MONOCLE COMMENT: **Å**boulevard is
a major transport thoroughfare so
we suggest requesting a room at the
back of the property for the most
peaceful night's sleep.

Visual tour

Avenue Hotel Copenhagen
invited local Instagrammers
to create artworks for the
hotel by photographing their
favourite places in the city.
Each image on display has a
QR code: visitors can scan
them with their smartphones
to reveal where each scenic
spot is located.

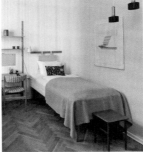

(7)
Hotel Alexandra, City Centre
Stay in a design museum

Under the management of the
passionate Jeppe Mühlhausen,
the Hotel Alexandra is a temple to
Danish Modern design – so much
so that a few nights there almost
negate the need to visit the Design
Museum. That's a very conscious
decision by Mühlhausen, who since
2001 has been stocking every room
of the hotel with covetable mid-
century pieces.

"I wanted to make a living
museum," he says. "We had a lot
of help from the Danish Architecture
School and I train the staff in the
history of the furniture."

The resulting spaces epitomise
Danish functionality and aesthetic
charm. While the smaller rooms
feature a range of items from a
variety of designers, the hotel also
has specialty suites dedicated solely
to the works of single creators,
including Hans J Wegner, Finn Juhl,
Arne Jacobsen and Nanna Ditzel.
"We get more and more guests
coming for a particular room,"
says Mühlhausen. Also worth a
look is the Collector's Suite, where
the furniture is refreshed every six
months and all the pieces on view
are also for sale.
8 HC Andersens Boulevard, 1553
+45 3374 4444
hotelalexandra.dk

to Alberto K restaurant on the 20th floor for breakfast with a view.
1 Hammerichsgade, 1611
+45 3342 6000
radissonblu.com

MONOCLE COMMENT: The hotel has undergone major renovations to refresh the fittings. However there is one room (*pictured*) that remains perfectly preserved and is the pick for anyone interested in the designs of Arne Jacobsen: Room 606 (*see page 110*). Be warned: you'll have to book well in advance.

⑨
Bella Sky Hotel, Ørestad
Dizzying heights

Of all the modern architecture in Copenhagen's Amager Vest district, Bella Sky Hotel's fan-like towers are a stand-out example – if only in height. These 76.5-metre colossi were designed in 2011 by Danish firm 3XN. The 812 rooms are just as futuristic as the exteriors – but furniture by Danish staples such as Hay gives them a homely touch. From the top-floor concertina bridge the towers' dramatic 15-degree incline is all the more impressive; head to the Sky Bar for a fiery chilli daiquiri and views over the natural reserve of Amager Common.
5 Center Boulevard, 2300
+45 3247 3000
acbellaskycopenhagen.dk

⑧
Radisson Blu Royal Hotel, Vesterbro
Trendsetting heritage

It's hard to miss the stark, somewhat unappealing exterior of the world's first designer hotel. Designed by modernist master Arne Jacobsen (*see page 108*), the 22-floor building first opened its doors in 1960. Jacobsen had a hand in designing every last detail and while the hotel has since been updated, some elements remain, such as the lounge chairs that were used in the passenger air terminal that operated in the hotel during the 1960s – they've been re-upholstered and are now dotted throughout the 260 guest rooms.

There's a well-equipped fitness centre as well as a dapper concierge who is always at the ready. For dining, we recommend heading up

I'm a literary figure: perhaps they'll name a suite after me too

⑩
Hotel d'Angleterre, City Centre
Stately style

The White Lady, as Hotel d'Angleterre is known, dates back to 1755. After a fire burnt down the original building in 1795, it moved to its current spot. This neoclassical palace was recently subject to a DKK500m (€67m) revamp and reopened in 2013. Undertaken by the charitable Remmen Foundation, the renovation was an "act of love" says foundation boardperson Elsa Marie Remmen. They aimed to make d'Angleterre feel like a "stylish but not stuffy stately residence".

Three of the 55 suites have a different theme – the Hans Christian Andersen suite has charming cut-outs the writer made in his downtime – and there are 37 good-sized rooms.

The foundation paid for a mostly Danish art collection as well as Andy Warhol's portrait of Queen Margrethe II. Come Christmas, thousands of lights on its façade turn it into a yuletide landmark.
34 Kongens Nytorv, 1050
+45 3312 0095
dangleterre.com

MONOCLE COMMENT: You don't have to be a guest to use the spa, where it seems sacrilegious to do laps in the pool's tranquil turquoise waters.

Historic lodgings

Hotel d'Angleterre grew out of a restaurant founded in the 17th century by Jean Marchal, a hairdresser who became a valet in the royal court, and Maria Coppy, daughter to the royal chef and an acclaimed cook in her own right. The pair added rooms in 1755 and the hotel was born.

Food and drink
—— Top tables

If you like to eat well and you like to eat stuff that you may not have tried before, you're lucky to be visiting Copenhagen now rather than 10 years ago. Few cities have transformed their food scene quite as radically and thoroughly, all starting with Noma.

The restaurant is still the best place in the world for New Nordic cuisine with its focus on local, seasonal produce, much of it foraged and a good deal of it pickled, dried, smoked or otherwise preserved for the long winters.

More recently the city's newly emboldened chefs and restaurateurs have begun to look further afield for influences and ingredients, allowing them to embrace previously shunned styles and produce from elsewhere in the world. Now there's great ramen, authentic Mexican food and better street food than the usual hot dog (although they too can be good), something especially welcome in what can still be quite a costly city for diners.

Restaurants
Where to eat

Growing trend
Dine in a greenhouse on a rooftop at ØsterGro

① Stedsans ØsterGro, Østerbro
Green party

One of the toughest reservations to secure in this city is at this greenhouse in a 600 sq m urban farm on the rooftop of an old warehouse. The fixed five-course menu is served to share between 24 guests who dine together at one table, lending a meal the convivial feel of a quirky dinner party.

The restaurant is open from April to October but happily the founders, wife and husband Mette Helbaek and Flemming Hansen, recently opened a year-round stall at Torvehallerne (*see page 36*) where you can try their organic/biodynamic main courses.
4 Aebelogade, 2100
cleansimplelocal.com

②
Pluto, City Centre
Stellar dining

This loud, lively and centrally located restaurant has a New Yorkish feel to it. That's partly down to the mix of seating (either at tables or on bar stools) and an open kitchen featuring lots of white tiles and raw concrete. And then there's the menu, which is based in France but still has licence to roam the rest of the globe (stopping off at WD50 and David Chang's Momofuku empire for inspiration), and which readily lends itself to the small-plates menu concept.

Always packed, Pluto is run by much-loved local chef Rasmus Oubaek, who seems to have a knack for knowing how Copenhageners like to dine. That means lots of super-savoury, smoky, cured meats, patés and charcuterie, as well as mountains of foie gras, decent cocktails, loud music and popular natural wines.
16 Borgergade, 1300
+45 3316 0016
restaurantpluto.dk

Bowl you over
—
The city has been rather late to the ramen phenomenon but brew gurus Mikkeller and Sapporo chef Takuro Otani have opened two surprisingly authentic spots (in Nørrebro and Vesterbro) serving eight different bowls plus beers. Our pick is the *yuzu* ramen.
ramentobiiru.dk

Must-try
Pea bygotto from Grød, citywide
The popularity of the four Grød restaurants has brought Danish all-hours porridge to the world. There's a host of grain-based bowls to try; our pick is the risotto-like bygotto made from pearl barley and served with peas and greens.
groed.com

Noma

Noma didn't just kick-start the New Nordic food movement: it also helped awaken the Danes' appetite for decent food and alerted them to the amazing produce on their doorstep. Numerous Noma alumni now operate in venues throughout Copenhagen – Amass, Bror, Hija de Sanchez, Studio and Relae, to name a few – but its influence has reached high-end restaurants around the globe.

Co-owned by chef René Redzepi, it is repeatedly named the best restaurant in the world. Noma is set to close in February/March 2017, reopening around October of that year as part of a new urban farm on the outskirts of Christiania. The idea is to offer an even more seasonal menu with greater emphasis on vegetables, many of them grown on-site.

Wherever Noma opens though, a reservation will always be tricky to secure. The standard method is to go online at 10.00 on the first Monday of the month for a shot at a table three months hence. But it's arguably worth taking a chance on what is, for many, a life-changing experience, and turning up on the day in the hope of a cancellation.
noma.dk

A growing business

Ex-Noma head chef Matt Orlando cultivates as many of his ingredients as possible in raised beds at the front of his Amass restaurant. The menu uses seasonal, often foraged produce, like cod roe, oats, and beach herbs.
amassrestaurant. com

③ Bror, City Centre
Innovative and impeccable

We could probably fill this guide with René Redzepi protégés who have spread their wings to open places elsewhere, but special mention must go to Brit Sam Nutter and Swede Viktor Wagram, who opened Bror on a shoestring in 2013. For all the "let's put on a show in the barn" vibe (as evoked by the mismatched crockery), there is genuine innovation and impeccable technique at work. They use the best Danish produce and pair it with plenty of natural wines in this tiny split-level space in Pisserenden, the city's studenty Latin Quarter.
24A Sankt Peders Straede, 1453
+45 3217 5999
bror-ante.dk

④ Almanak, City Centre
Save the date

Claus Meyer's Almanak is one of three restaurants in The Standard building, with Studio upstairs (*see page 29*) and Indian restaurant Verandah. It has a more basic menu than Studio and as you'd expect from the godfather of the Nordic food movement, the fare is strictly seasonal and local, so you'll find excellent *smørrebrød* and updated, unfussy Danish classics such as juniper-smoked salmon, neck of lamb and organic chicken, all served in a high-ceilinged dining room with waterfront views.
44 Havnegade, 1058
+45 7214 8808
thestandardcph.dk

Hey, a leaf. I could forage that for a New Nordic meal

5

108, Christianshavn
Deceptively casual

108 opened its doors in mid-2016 and grew out of a plan hatched by René Redzepi (*see page 26*) and former Relæ sous chef Kristian Baumann (*see pages 28 and 79*) over coffee. "We had similar ideas of what a casual restaurant could look like," says Baumann. "We wanted people to spend time diving into the food and we wanted to trigger their memories." The restaurant's floor-to-ceiling windows look onto the Christianshavn canals and the kitchen serves New Nordic flavours with an international bent, including bread miso soup.
108 Strandgade, 1401
+45 3296 3292
108.dk

Must-try
Flødeboller from
Lagkagehuset, citywide
These lumpy traditional Danish treats may be inelegantly shaped but they taste good. The most common iteration is a chocolate-coated meringue filling sitting on a wafer or marzipan base.
lagkagehuset.dk

6

Havfruen, City Centre
Catch of the day

The latest venture from Frederik Bille Brahe of Café Atelier September (*see page 37*), Havfruen translates as "mermaid" – but in case you missed the reference, there's a huge wooden sculpture of one reclining over the bar. The dark, moody interior is an antidote to Nyhavn's more touristy attractions, serving Frederik's signature vegetarian meals but also adding seafood to the mix (most of which is sourced from a local fisherman). Dessert fans should make a point of checking out the Bleeding Chocolate Cake with avocado ice cream and matcha.
39 Nyhavn, 1051
+45 3311 1138
restaurantthavfruen.dk

⑦
Relae, Nørrebro
No compromises

These days the idea of a bare-table, no-frills restaurant serving refined conceptual food is nothing unusual – but Relae was one of the first. Its Norwegian-Italian-Danish founder, chef Christian Puglisi, doesn't know the meaning of the word "compromise". This can mean challenging flavours and textures but mostly a meal will be one to remember. "Poverty" ingredients such as celeriac and mackerel are turned into dishes worthy of the kind of silver-cloche reveal you'd never see at Relae. Instead, the theatricality comes from the produce.
41 Jaegersborggade, 2200
+45 3696 6609
restaurant-relae.dk

Pony, Vesterbro
Informal dining

The original site of Kadeau *(see page 29)*, this is now a less formal, lower-price venue from the same Bornholm culinary innovators. While they still serve modern Nordic-style dishes – often using foraged herbs, local seafood and organic meats – and a selection of intriguing natural wines, there's now more of a local restaurant vibe to the place. Take a seat at the counter and enjoy dishes such as salt cod with oyster vinaigrette and veal sweetbreads with wild garlic.
135 Vesterbrogade, 1620
+45 3322 1000
ponykbh.dk

Baest bet
——
Try a sharing plate for a taste of everything

⑨
Baest, Nørrebro
Well worth the wait

Baest opened in 2014 to queues literally around the block, and has maintained that level of popularity ever since thanks to impeccable wood-fired sourdough pizzas, dazzling in-house charcuterie (the super-rich pork rillettes are hauntingly good), organic mozzarella made fresh in the dairy upstairs every day and a big-city atmosphere. The city's best cinema, the Empire, is just across the way, while Baest's sister venue, the excellent Mirabelle bakery and café, is next door, its fresh pasta of the day a recent popular innovation.
29 Guldbergsgade, 2200
+45 3535 0463
baest.dk

⑪
Brus/Restaurant Spontan, Nørrebro
Tap into this

Brus packs a lot into its 750 sq m site, once home to a locomotive factory. The clean-lined decor of the brewpub owes much to its 13 fermentation tanks and 70 oak casks containing To Øl's repertoire of barrel-aged brews. Drinks are served from a nine-metre-long bar with no fewer than 33 taps, and while snacks are available, the real food is produced at Restaurant Spontan, with which Brus shares space.

Featuring one of Denmark's youngest Michelin-starred chefs – Christian Gadient – in the kitchen, there are no signature dishes on offer here. Spontan literally means "spontaneous" and Gadient turned his back on the fine-dining scene when this space opened in 2016 so he could make the most of the freedom to focus on creating new flavours.

29F Guldbergsgade, 2200
+45 7522 2200
tapperietbrus.dk

Must-try
Pulled pork burger from Oink Oink at Copenhagen Street Food
Roast pork is practically a national dish in Denmark (the country is among the world's leading producers of porcine products). This slow-cooked tangy treat comes with chipotle chilli sauce and a slice of pickle.
oinkoink.dk

⑩
Kadeau, Christianshavn
Modern comforts

From their origins on the Baltic island of Bornholm, the Kadeau team have brought a welcome warmth and brazen deliciousness to New Nordic's sometimes rather "hair shirt" ethos: contemporary yet comforting food is the order of the day here.

Located in a gorgeous new home, which boasts warm wooden surfaces and a garden view, the restaurant is pricey but the superb seafood, richly flavoured organic pork and chicken – and great Bornholm-grown vegetables – are worth it.

10B Wildersgade, 1408
+45 3325 2223
kadeau.dk

Forbidden fruits
————
Torsten Vildgaard won a Michelin star within four months of opening Studio. His cuisine is rooted in the Danish soil but he's also unafraid to inject ingredients previously frowned upon by the New Nordic manifesto, such as foie gras and truffles.
thestandardcph.dk

⑫
Spise\Bar Nr 20, Nørrebro
Without borders

In 2014 Tanya-Maria Solskov transformed a rundown bodega on a Nørrebro backstreet into a cosy wood-panelled neighbourhood haunt. "She wanted it to be a restaurant where diners could share food, enjoy cocktails and drink good wine," says head chef Arek Jensen. Besides the tapas, Jensen's weekly menu includes two dishes: one meat and one vegetarian. "Our cooking is New Nordic but with a multicultural twist," he says. From jerk chicken with corn purée and popcorn to gazpacho with goat's cheese, the changing menu warrants multiple visits.
20 Rantzausgade, 2200
+45 3536 0290

Folkekøkken

The *Folkekøkken* is the Danish solution to the problem of low-income dining: communal kitchens offering simple, quality meals to large numbers of diners for about DKK50 (€7) per person, usually one or two nights of the week.

Tuesday is the big day for these "People's Kitchens", many of which are in Nørrebro and Vesterbro. The menus tend, for obvious reasons, to be basic. Some, like Café Le Rouge in Nørrebro, have higher ambitions and might serve marinated chicken or goulash, for example. Others are vegetarian or vegan, like the one at Dortheavej 61 in the Nordvest quarter. The former Meatpacking District has Folkekøkken Vesterbro but probably the most famous is Absalon, which serves daily from 18.00. The culinary standard is so high (a good example of a typical serving is its *aeggekaen*, a kind of raised omelette, with leek, gruyere and mozzarella) that it has been favourably reviewed by the restaurant critics in Denmark's national newspapers.
cafelerouges.dk;
dortheavej-61.dk;
folkekøkken-vesterbro.dk;
absaloncph.dk

Lucky I brought my bib: I'm ready for Oink Oink's epic burger

(13)
Geist, City Centre
High-end trends

Danes can be suspicious of dressy restaurants so this chic, low-lit venue is about as snazzy as things get in the capital. Grab a counter seat and watch the kitchen team, led by Danish celeb chef Bo Bech, add a luxe touch to Nordic produce and wider-ranging ingredients such as *yuzu*, piment d'espelette and octopus (which Danes rarely eat outside tapas bars). Bech keeps up with leading chefs around the world so this is a good place to follow high-end dining trends, plus he is unafraid of unexpected pairings: stilton and chocolate, anyone?
8 Kongens Nytorv, 1050
+45 3313 3713
restaurantgeist.dk

(14)
Geranium, City Centre
Gold-medal fare

You might imagine Geranium's chef Rasmus Kofoed *(below)* to be rather intense. He won a bronze statue at the "chef Olympics", the Bocuse d'Or, followed up with silver and gold, then became the first Danish chef to bag three Michelin stars. His intensity goes into his food, which has a sublime delicacy, lightness and refinement. This kind of modernist Nordic multi-course blow out – using biodynamic meat where possible and local seafood and vegetables – is not for everyone (or their wallet) but in his sphere Kofoed is at the top of his game.
4 Per Henrik Lings Allé, 2100
+45 6996 0020
geranium.dk

Meatpacking District
Tasty fillet of dining spots

(1)
Gorilla, Vesterbro
Go bananas

The Meatpacking District (Kødbyen) isn't short of cool places to eat and drink but this recent venue from the team behind Pluto *(see page 25)* really exploits the open plan of what was once the Karriere Bar (and before that used for meat processing) to create a funky, relaxed atmosphere perfect for their punchily flavoured small plates. The 15-dish snack menu may be a little excessive so try the 10-course option, which roams a familiar "dirty gourmet" repertoire of brisket sliders, lobster rolls, Korean hot dogs and pig-tail chips.
63 Flæsketorvet, 1711
+45 3333 8330
restaurantgorilla.dk

Saucy beasts
—
Warpigs offers four punchy table sauces

②
Warpigs Brewpub, Vesterbro
Pig out

This raucous brewpub has been a welcome recent addition to the bustling Meatpacking District. It combines an enjoyably chaotic Texan barbecue (you queue up for your meat, which is served on sheets of brown paper, and then head off to find your own seating) with a range of 20 fantastic beers produced in collaboration between US brewer 3Floyds and local Mikkeller (*see page 41*).

The meat itself – ribs, brisket, pulled pork – is smoked for 12 to 14 hours until it falls apart if you so much as look at it, and is served by weight. If that's not enough to sate your appetite there are naughty sides of mac'n'cheese and burnt baked beans available, plus a range of pickles and sauces.

25-37 Flaesketorvet, 1711
+45 4348 4848
warpigs.dk

Twin passions
—
Mikkeller beer founder Mikkel Borg Bjergsø has an identical twin brother who is also in the business. Jeppe Jarnit-Bjergsø owns a boutique brewery in Brooklyn and the name of his enterprise is a nod to the apparently fraught relationship between the two: Evil Twin Brewing.

③
Hija de Sanchez, Vesterbro
Taco belle

Chicago-born Rosio Sanchéz already had a reputation as one of the most innovative and respected pastry chefs in the world when she opened an "as authentic as I can make it" taqueria stand at Torvhallerne. Her three tacos for DKK100 (€13.50) offer was such a success (the Nordic-influenced El Paul with crispy fish skin and gooseberry salsa is amazing) that she opened a permanent indoor space here. It is still focused on takeaway tacos (made with masa from imported Mexican corn), *paletas* (Mexican ice lollies) and Mexican-style cheese and drinks.
8 Slagterboderne, 1716
hijadesanchez.dk

④
Kødbyens Fiskebar, Vesterbro
No ordinary fish bar

"Our food is local and playful; it's created to delight and excite," says Fiskebar's Michelin-trained head chef Jamie Lee. And it's easy to see his expert hand at work in the dishes here. This is no ordinary fish and chips: using seasonal vegetables and foraged ingredients to complement top-notch seafood, he turns out favourites such as trout tartare with rye emulsion, capers and burnt onion, or scallops, peas, wild mushrooms and anchovy. It's also one of the best places to enjoy a summer evening – staff set up deckchairs in the carpark out front.
100 Flaesketorvet, 1711
+45 3215 5656
fiskebaren.dk

⑤
Kul, Vesterbro
Nordic taste odyssey

No, it's not an abbreviation of "cool", although the matte-black interiors do exude an altogether different type of slick aesthetic to the wooden furnishings found in most other restaurants. Kul is Danish for "coal", a fitting name for a kitchen favouring a charcoal yakitori grill and Josper griddle.

Head chef and founder Henrik Jyrk opened the restaurant in 2013 following his jaunt through the best dining rooms and kitchens on the US's West Coast. The mix of flavours, however, isn't prescribed solely to Californian sensibilities. Highlights include wild prawns with spicy avocado, and beef tenderloin with porcini mushroom and smoked scallops. Vegetarians may have to skip straight to dessert but they won't be disappointed.
16B-20 Høkerboderne, 1712
+45 3321 0033
restaurantkul.dk

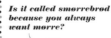

Is it called smørrebrød because you always want mørre?

Paté Paté, Vesterbro
Packing them in

In a prime position on a corner site at the entrance to the Meatpacking District, Paté Paté has become one of the hottest tickets in Copenhagen so don't expect to just saunter up and snag a table. It's a bustling, noisy place where the staff are run off their feet, which should clue you in to the popularity of the fare.

The menu is inspired by recipes from France, Spain and Morocco, with owner Kenn Husted travelling to those countries several times a year for inspiration. One of the most popular dishes is onglet, a cut of beef favoured in France, while whole pig's head has also proven a hit. And there's paté, although that's not the source of the restaurant's name. "The space used to be a paté factory," says Husted. "We doubled the word to indicate two brothers joining forces to start a business."
1 Slagterboderne, 1716
+45 3969 5557
patepate.dk

Food markets and shops
Homegrown goods

1
Løgismose, City Centre
One-stop shop

This spacious gourmet supermarket was once the only place in Copenhagen to buy decent foreign cheeses, charcuterie and wines. Today the Løgismose brand has products in supermarkets across the country but its flagship (still the only place to get proper Normandy butter) is a great place to grab French, Spanish and Italian *delikatesser* and quality wines.
16 Nordre Toldbod, 1259
+45 3332 9332
loegismose.dk

Harbour eats
Take your pick of the food vans and bag a spot

②
Copenhagen Street Food, Papirøen
Printing menus

Here's a pragmatic Scandinavian solution to the weather in these parts: put your food trucks indoors, in this case in a former newspaper warehouse on the harbourfront. A world of fast food is now under one roof, from butter chicken and bibimbap, to pulled duck burgers, falafel and tacos. Take your pick and find a table outside, with a glass of something chilled in hand, for one of the best harbour views in the city. A bonus: the bridge from Nyhavn to Christianshavn has finally opened, making access from the city centre a snap.
Warehouse 7&8
14 Transgravsvej, 1436
copenhagenstreetfood.dk

Let's pop over to Papirøen for a romantic taco

(3)

Torvehallerne, City Centre
Market force

Opening in 2011 on the site of the old fruit and veg market on Israels Plads, these two glass halls became a focal point for food. Inside, and in the outdoor public spaces between the two, is a culinary cornucopia: fresh fish, meat, fruit and vegetables; Italian, Spanish, Asian, French and Bornholmsk delicacies; takeaways from Gorm's pizza and Coffee Collective; and Italian ice cream, posh chocolate, tea and cake (though perhaps there are too many healthy eating/juice bar places). Be sure to stop by the brilliant taqueria, Hija de Sanchez and Stedsans stalls.

21 Frederiksborggade, 1360
torvehallernekbh.dk

Sweet obsessions

Johan Bülow turned his passion for quality liquorice into the global brand Lakrids, going from his mother's kitchen to the likes of Fortnum & Mason's in London. Find the full Lakrids range in the food hall of Magasin du Nord.
lakrids.nu

Hot dogs

When the Danes need a quick snack they head for one of the city centre's many mobile hot-dog wagons. Most are perfectly serviceable, but the best are run by DØP. It has two vans stationed by the Round Tower on the pedestrian shopping street Købmagergade, and outside Helligåndskirken on Strøget. DØP's hot dogs are a cut above (spicy beef sausage with root veg mash, for example) and all-organic. It even does a vegetarian option.
doep.dk

Brunch and lunch
Early options

①
Aamanns Deli & Take Away,
City Centre
Rye smiles

Chef Adam Aamann has made his
name by updating the archetypal
Danish lunch staple *smørrebrød*
(open sandwiches), through the
use of high-quality local produce
such as free-range pork and
chicken, and locally grown seasonal
vegetables. But more than the
sandwich contents themselves,
as Aamann is quick to point out,
it's the rye bread that forms the
foundation of any good *smørrebrød*.
His rye bread takes two days to
make and is rich, malty and sour
– just as it should be.
10 Oster Farimagsgade, 2100
+45 3555 3344
aamanns.dk

②
Café Atelier September, City Centre
Simple pleasures

Chef Frederik Bille Brahe
(*pictured*) opened his café on
the premises of Gothersgade
boutique Atelier September in
2013. Since then the former head
chef of renowned Saison has
busied himself creating simple but
exceptional vegetarian meals. But
what really sets this café apart is
the quirky decision not to include
a kitchen – the food is prepared on
standalone steel tables and a single
induction plate.

The space itself is light and airy
and is a favourite with the brunch
crowd; you should sample the
café's signature dish, an open-faced
sandwich of thinly sliced avocado
on rye. The yoghurt granola with
zucchini and matcha tea is another
hit, scoring almost as highly for
presentation as for taste. Brahe is
also behind Havfruen restaurant
(*see page 27*).
30 Gothersgade, 1123
cafeatelierseptember.com

*No kitchen? At
least there's a
coffee machine*

③
Møller Kaffe & Køkken, Nørrebro
The pleasure principle

This modern Scandinavian café in a former bank building designed by none other than Arne Jacobsen was recently voted the best brunch place in the city. It won for its contemporary *hygge* (relaxing and pleasurable) interior of concrete floors, modern Danish sofas, mismatched raw wood tables and counter, and its food by chef Andreas Møller, who has experience at numerous refined venues. Choose from 25 options including homemade Nutella, and pork from organic specialist Spis min gris (Eat my pig).

160 Nørrebrogade, 2200
+45 3150 5100
kaffeogkoekken.dk

Oh, schnapp
There are over 140 kinds of schnapps here

④
Restaurant Schønnemann, City Centre
Traditional favourite

The unanimous choice of Copenhagen's chefs for the city's best *smørrebrød* (open sandwich), this posh cellar dates back to 1877. While it looks every inch the traditional Danish lunch restaurant, the quality of ingredients is what sets Schønnemann's apart.

Start with one of the herring options, then try smoked eel or a Bettina's Favourite: braised pork belly with demiglace and rhubarb. A taste of one of the 140 different schnapps is obligatory. Open for lunch only.

16 Hauser Plads, 1127
+45 3312 0785
restaurantschonnemann.dk

Too many
smørrebrød.
Worth it,
however...

Bakeries
Danish pastries

② Lagkagehuset, citywide
Flødeboller fancies

This quality bakery chain has grown rapidly, thanks to its consistently great, mostly organic breads (they let their sourdough proof for 48 hours and have 10 types of rye), coffee and cakes. The toasted cheese and ham sandwiches are utterly addictive, and be sure to try the giant flødeboller, Denmark's answer to the Walnut Whip.
lagkagehuset.dk

Three more bakeries

01 Andersen Bakery, citywide: The Andersen Bakery chain was actually founded in Japan long before opening in Denmark, to sell authentic Danish pastries and breads back to the Danes with great success. The main branch is located across from the main entrance to Central Station.
andersen-danmark.dk

02 Meyers Deli, citywide Another arm of the Claus Meyer food empire, these inviting delicatessens and cafés specialise in great sourdough and rye bread, sandwiches and coffee. They stock the full range of Meyer's other food products too, notably his fruit vinegars, juices and jams. Branches can be found in the basement of department store Magasin du Nord and elsewhere.
meyersmad.dk

03 La Glace, City Centre: This shop was founded in 1870 which makes it one of the oldest bakeries in Denmark. It serves super-indulgent layer cakes and pastries (and a great hot chocolate) in its evocative space filled with 19th-century furniture, just off Strøget.
laglace.dk

① Emmerys, citywide
Leading the way

Emmerys revolutionised Copenhagen's bakery scene in the early 2000s with its cakes, organic juices, dark-roasted Arabica coffee, sourdough bread and Dean & DeLuca-style takeaway salads, soups and sandwiches. All are served in contemporary wood-and-stone Scandinavian interiors.
emmerys.dk

Drinks
Beers and wines

① Ved Stranden, City Centre
Try before you buy

With an interior of Danish design classics, interesting wines from smaller growers (mostly French but also further afield to the New World) and a much-loved Monday-night tradition in which a guest chef serves a one-pot "staff meal", this is the wine bar of your dreams.

Sommelier Christian Nedergaard will happily let you try his more challenging natural wines before you commit to a glass, plus there is a selection of cheese and charcuterie to soak up the booze. Indeed, the food at Ved Stranden has been such a success that Nedergaard and his team opened a new restaurant in 2016 in a former theatre at Admiralgade 26 (also the venue's name); it serves a mostly organically sourced menu and a shorter but perfectly formed wine list.
10 Ved Stranden, 1061
+45 3542 4040
vedstranden10.dk

② Lidkoeb, Vesterbro
Laidback libations

This super-*hyggeligt* (that's Danish for "cosy") three-storey cocktail bar is hidden in a courtyard behind Føtex supermarket on Vesterbro's high street. It is a cocoon of natural materials, with wood and leather furniture draped with Faroese sheep skins, plus candles and an open fire, for a more relaxed feel than the city's more dressy addresses.

It's a place for grown-ups, with cocktails – both classics and in-house specials (we like the ones using herbs such as basil and sage) – and a whisky bar with more than 200 bottles in the rafters on the top floor.
72B Vesterbrogade, 1620
+45 3311 2010
lidkoeb.dk

This is how I drink in a little Danish history

Liquid trade
Wines are delivered by boat to Den Vandrette

③
Ruby, City Centre
Hidden gem

As with Lidkoeb *(see page 40)*, which is run by the same team, part of the pleasure of a visit to Ruby is in finding the place. In this case it is located, speakeasy-style, on the first floor of an 18th-century canal-front townhouse in the City Centre (coincidentally where the Dansk Spiritus Kompagni was founded in 1882).

Ruby peddles a distinctively Scandinavian-style of relaxed glamour, complete with Chesterfield sofas and an unexpected outdoor courtyard terrace that is particularly lovely in the late afternoon when it's less crowded. The cocktails available here change along with the seasons and have their basis in artisan liqueurs and homemade fruit syrups; just another reason why this place frequently shows up on lists of the best bars from around the world.
10 Nybrogade, 1203
+45 3393 1203
rby.dk

④
Den Vandrette, City Centre
Wine sail

Wine importers Rosforth & Rosforth – the folks behind this chic basement wine bar on the harbour near Nyhavn – are absolutely fanatical about natural, organic and biodynamic wines. Their passion is completely consuming, to the extent that they have many of their wines delivered to the wine bar by sailing ship, the thinking being that this helps to "minimise the impact of the journey".

As far as food is concerned, Den Vandrette also serves a (usually French) dish of the day, plus there's charcuterie and cheese.
53A Havnegade, 1058
+45 7214 8228
denvandrette.dk

⑤
Mikkeller Bar, Vesterbro
Something's brewing

A pioneer of the collaborative "gypsy" brewing phenomenon, Mikkeller (a conflation of the names of its founders, Mikkel Borg Bjergso and Kristian Keller) is now a global brand with outposts from San Francisco to Bangkok, and more than 800 different beers under its belt. It all started at this café-style space in a light, white basement in Vesterbro. Friendly staff serve an ever-changing range of 20 often surprising/weird brews. You can also pick up some of the brand's vibrantly packaged beverages at their Torvehallerne shop.
8B-C Viktoriagade, 1655
+45 3331 0415
mikkeller.dk

Chic makeover

Strøm replaced an old Irish pub

(6)
Strøm Bar, City Centre
Shake it up

This cosy cocktail bar opened in 2012 in its basement location just off Copenhagen's loveliest square, Gråbrødretorv. And while it may sound somewhat nerdy to specialise in recreating historical cocktails, Strøm's Swedish brothers Andreas and Mikael Nilsson do it with great style against a lovely art deco backdrop.

With some of the duo's alcoholic creations available on tap, the great bane of the cocktail drinker – the wait for that first sip – is minimised. In summer enjoy your drinks on benches outside on the cobbles.
32 Niels Hemmingsensgade, 1153
+45 8118 9421
strombar.dk

(1)
The Coffee Collective, Nørrebro
Bean around

Founded by four top baristas, The Coffee Collective was one of the first to emphasise ethical beans and quality processing. "We wanted to show how well coffee could be sourced, roasted and brewed," says co-owner Klaus Thomsen.

The roaster and a new café are located in Frederiksberg but the original tiny space in Nørrebro is still a top pick: the lack of a counter between the customers and the staff working the Probat roaster and espresso machine creates an intimate, homely vibe for observing the action on lively Jaegersborggade.
10 Jaegersborggade, 2200
+45 6015 1525
coffeecollective.dk

②
Democratic Coffee, City Centre
Coffee for the people

Following a woeful cup of coffee
served in the Københavns
Biblioteker café, Oliver Oxfeldt
put a business plan together, won
the tender to take over the space
and left his job in the gaming
industry. That was back in 2011;
now his aptly named Democratic
Coffee – a nod to the million
patrons who pass through the
public library's doors each year
– has developed a formidable
following for perfectly poured
coffees and fresh flaky pastries.

The single-origin beans are
roasted by the Democratic Coffee
team and the crisp croissants are
baked in-house using a technique
Oxfeldt claims he learnt from a
YouTube video. Great coffee paired
with the calm of the neighbouring
library make for a cosy pit-stop,
particularly when the weather is
less than ideal.
15 Krystalgade, 1172
+45 4019 6237

③
Prolog Coffee Bar, Vesterbro
Packed with creativity

Enthusiastic baristas and roasters
Sebastian Quistorff Sørensen and
Jonas Gehl opened Prolog in the
Meatpacking District in 2016. "We
love the innovative and creative
chaos that exists here," says Sørensen.

The dynamic area is a fitting petri
dish for their experiments with the
bean. Even their food uses it: try the
coffee hot sauce (a collaboration
with the city's famous purveyor
of sausages in a bun, John's
Hotdog Deli), or the olive-
and-coffee chocolate bars. The
marshmallows that customers
roast themselves over small grills
are another crowd pleaser.
16 Høkerboderne, 1712
+45 3125 5675

④
Café Det Vide Hus, City Centre
Home brews

Inspired by the ambience of Harvey
Keitel's tobacco shop in the movie
Smoke, owner Claus Dalsgaard
opened this coffee house to appeal to
all walks of life. The fact that it's more
than held its own against the city's
larger coffee chains suggests that the
plan has worked. The chatty, laidback
atmosphere feels more like someone's
home than a café – better yet, it's
a home where no one minds if you
put your feet up on the furniture.

"Over the years our many
regulars have made the café their
own, each in their way," says
Dalsgaard. "Of course we want to
make amazing coffee but ultimately
everything tastes better when you
unwind in good company."

The staff eschew gimmicks yet
stay on top of the latest in barista
best practice (Dalsgaard helped
pioneer the pour-over and aeropress
in Copenhagen). If you fancy a
nibble there's bread and croissants,
both baked in-house.
113 Gothersgade, 1123

Retail
—— Something old, something new

①
Stine Goya, City Centre
Bold geometrics

The Danes' innate sense of style and long history of homegrown design talent make Copenhagen a true world leader when it comes to retail. Whether it's homeware and furniture by industry luminaries such as Georg Jensen and Gubi Olsen, or innovative fashion from a new generation including Legends and Stine Goya, you'll be covered for new threads and house revamps. And, of course, no trip would be complete without a browse of the iconic Danish Modern furniture in the antique shops and auction houses. Then there are the specialist bicycle-makers, café-cum-record shops and the Lego flagship. As most retailers are within walking distance, the city is very shoppable indeed. We recommend arriving with an empty suitcase.

"I want to inspire and stimulate women to express themselves through playful, artistic and intellectual design," says Stine Goya (*pictured, right*), who first gained attention in Denmark when she took home the Dansk Fashion Award for 2011 designer of the year.

Goya set up her namesake label in 2006 and opened a shop eight years later on the bustling Gothersgade. Her signature geometric prints, bold accessories and bright colour palettes are tempered by easy cuts that channel the archetypal simplicity of Scandinavian design.
58 Gothersgade, 1123
+45 3217 1000
stinegoya.com

I look pretty fly? Thank you. Coming from you that means a lot.

2

Black, Frederiksberg
Precious porcelain

When potter Anne Black was
considering opening a shop to
sell her porcelain, she felt endless
shelves of ceramics might look
dull. "The room needed to be
a universe of beautiful things," she
says. Accordingly, in the corner lot
she created in 2013, you'll find a
thoughtful curation of womenswear,
homeware and furniture, most of
which is made by hand. "I like to
carry niche brands you can't find
on every corner," adds Black. She
also runs Black Studio a few doors
down, hosting pop-ups by local
designers and artists.
105 Gammel Kongevej, 1850
+45 3321 7799
blackcph.com

The new black
—
Anne's shop
carries more
than just
porcelain

Precious purl
—
Artist and textile designer
Signe Emdal founded Emdal
Studio in 2007 after working
for Henrik Vibskov. Her label
offers scarves, capes and
blankets, all produced
in her Amager workshop on
a 1984 German Jacquard
knitting machine.
emdalstudio.com

③ Yvonne Koné, City Centre
Back to basics

Designer Yvonne Koné describes her effortlessly chic accessories as "simple favourites that only get better with time". A graduate of the Royal Danish Academy of Fine Arts, she established her business in 2011. Today she collaborates with traditional Italian artisans: a family-run factory produces her leather bags, and her cashmere scarves are woven at a workshop using early 20th-century looms.

Koné's small but beautifully arranged space in the city centre – a former antiques shop transformed for her by design consultant Oliver Gustav – is ideal for the colour-coordinated pieces. Bags, clutches and purses hang on iron rails, while shoes, boots and sandals perch on grey-toned shelves that match the walls.
3 Store Strandstraaede, 1255
+45 3220 4400
yvonnekone.com

④ Cecilie Copenhagen, City Centre
Comfortable cottons

It takes some sleuthing to find this shop (when you see the flight of wonky wooden stairs you're on the right track). The signature shorts and T-shirts from Cecilie Jørgensen's womenswear business had humble beginnings. "I made the shorts using my dad's old underpants as a template," says Jørgensen, with a laugh. Since the initial 2011 line, the range has grown to include trousers, dresses and jackets. The comfortable, versatile threads are spun from Italian, Indian and Portuguese cottons.
3F, 13 Valkendorfsgade, 1153
ceciliecopenhagen.com

⑤ Holly Golightly, City Centre
Edgy threads

Barbara Werner left the film industry to open a luxury women's boutique in 2001. Back then the city had limited avant garde offerings so she set out to stock Proenza Schouler, Rick Owens and, later, Stine Goya *(see page 44)* and Freya Dalsjø. "I find an eclectic mix of things more compelling than just one brand," she says. "I also like something that doesn't lose momentum, designers that don't go out of fashion." Her selection of independent imprints and her own knitwear range spans two shops; accessories and shoes are stocked on Store Regnegade.
2 Gammel Mønt, 1117
+45 3314 1915
hollygolightly.dk

1
Soulland, Frederiksberg
Contemporary cool

Creative director Silas Adler was just 17 years old when he launched Soulland in 2002. Four years later, Jacob Kampp Berliner's arrival as a co-owner sparked a fruitful creative partnership that has seen the pair turn out four collections a year ever since. They specialise in contemporary reworkings of menswear classics, many of which are made in Copenhagen. Their baseball cap and fedora hybrid (in other words, a felt hat with a cap brim) has become a signature product.

A commission from Post Danmark to produce a one-off stamp was followed by Adler being named the country's designer of the year back in 2012. Both events have helped to establish Soulland as one of the country's pre-eminent fashion offerings.
41 Gammel Kongevej, 1610
+45 5364 0186
soulland.com

2
Han Kjøbenhavn, City Centre
Homegrown inspiration

The people behind this menswear retailer make clothes they believe are quintessentially Scandinavian – but also pride themselves on their points of difference. "We have an interest in Danish design, architecture and furniture but our roots are in the suburbs, so we've maintained our identity," says co-founder Jannik Wikkelsø Davidsen.

Sleek denim hangs next to Finn Juhl coffee-table books, sweatpants, tracksuits and Portuguese jersey jumpers. Don't leave without a pair of the firm's revered clip-on tortoiseshell sunglasses.
7 Vognmagergade, 1120
hankjobenhavn.com

3
Goods, Østerbro
From the bottom up

Kasper Hostrup's Goods launched in 2008 as a discreet basement emporium but quickly became a staple purveyor of men's fashion. The dignified shop resembles less a boutique and more a comely wardrobe. "We only sell what we love and respect," says Hostrup (*pictured above*) who oversees the selection from Aspesi chinos and Mismo luggage to Nanamica shirts and in-house label Capital Goods. There's also a small but polished line of womenswear and a range of books and independent magazines such as *Spis* and *Apartamento*.
44 Østerbrogade, 2100
+45 3543 0505
goodscph.com

Global name
——
The brand has outposts in Paris, LA and New York

④
Legends, City Centre
New kids on the block

Legends opened the door to its first shop in early 2016, joining a notable retail cohort on this inner-city shopping stretch, including Han Kjøbenhavn and Storm.

It was founded by Thomas Dam and Mads Ulrik Greenfort (*pictured below*) in 2013 and has gained traction for its impeccably tailored clothing and refined collection of trainers, boots and caps. Expect clean Scandinavian lines combined with laidback Californian style. The shop and the offices below are located in a heritage-listed building dating back to 1736.
35 Gammel Mønt, 1117
+45 3132 2322
legends.dk

Mixed fashion
Something for everyone

❶
Norse Store, City Centre
Skater style

Tobia Sloth, Anton Juul and Mikkel Grønnebaek shared a passion for skateboarding culture but outgrew its trademark look. In 2004, drawing on their architecture and design backgrounds, they set up Norse Projects as a space where they could bring international names to their hometown; by 2009 they had set up their own label of the same name. The outdoorwear and basics were a hit; the trio debuted a womenswear line in 2015 in Pilestraede. "We didn't want to be on a main street: people need to feel like they found the shop themselves," says Grønnebaek.

Accessories and shoes in collaboration with the likes of Dr. Martens sit on shelves made from repurposed Dinesen floorboards, while the brand's own pieces are interspersed with Comme des Garçons shirts and Visvim parkas.
41 Pilestraede, 1112
+45 3393 2626
norsestore.com

Department stores

01 **Illum, City Centre:** Opened in 1891, Illum was the capital's first department store. Stocked labels span home talent such as Mads Nørgaard and international offerings that include Loewe and Alexander Wang. Architect Claudio Silvestrin's 2015 revamp added a hotel and rooftop space. Not to be confused with Illums Bolighus (*see page 52*).
illum.dk

02 **Magasin du Nord, City Centre:** This retail behemoth on Kongens Nytorv caters to more democratic tastes (think Tiger and Hugo Boss), but the real reason to go is the renowned food court on the top floor.
magasin.dk

03 **Birger Christensen, City Centre:** J. Birger Christensen's eponymous shop features a selection of luxury fashion houses such as Tom Ford and Valentino, as well as the fur coats that Birger Christensen has been designing since 1869. A vast collection of the latter can be found hanging in the Danish royal wardrobe.
birger-christensen.com

I'm heading for Magasin du Nord's restaurant.

Wood Wood, City Centre
Primed for action

Wood Wood streetwear is an unofficial uniform in the city. Karl-Oskar Olsen and Brian SS Jensen are the men behind this cult brand, which they founded off the back of youths spent in the capital's graffiti and street-culture scene of the 1990s. They ply a sporty collection of high-end sweatshirts, trousers and trainers for men and women alike. The duo added denim to the line-up in 2015. Head to the flagship on Grønnegade, or peruse previous collections at the Wood Wood Museum on Frederiksborggade, opposite the lakes.
1 Grønnegade, 1107
+45 3535 6263
woodwood.com

Artistic display
——
Vibskov's shop is a theatrical backdrop

② Henrik Vibskov, City Centre
Ethically designed

The rotating decor inside Henrik Vibskov's Krystalgade shop is as fantastical as his clothing. "My collections are very conceptual; we try to work with installations and performance," says Vibskov, who graduated from London's Central Saint Martin's design school in 2001 and has since become one of the country's premier names in fashion. A portion of the men's and womenswear is manufactured in Denmark: the rest in Portugal and India. The house label is supplemented by Vibskov's favourite picks from Denmark and abroad.
6 Krystalgade, 1172
+45 3314 6100
henrikvibskov.com

Storm, City Centre
Lifestyle and fashion hub

Fashion designer Rasmus Storm launched his namesake shop in 1994 with a small premises in Nørrebro that stocked solely Scandinavian designers. In 2001 he moved to a bigger space in the city centre and now carries pieces by both emerging and established Danish designers, and international names such as Céline, Maison Kitsuné and Comme des Garçons.

Today a noted lifestyle and fashion shop, Storm has a clean concept feel. It stocks men's and womenswear – naturally, the latest trends – as well as beauty products, music, magazines, books and more. You're likely to find the latest issue of MONOCLE magazine here, as well as our books collection and Travel Guide Series, complete with the very book in your hands.
1 Store Regnegade, 1110
+45 3393 0014
stormfashion.dk

④

Andersen-Andersen, City Centre
Sea change

Partners Cathrine Lundgren-Andersen and Peter Kjaer-Andersen (*pictured above*) founded their business in order to reinterpret maritime knitwear. "It started when we bought an old, symmetrical sailor jumper," says Lundgren-Andersen. "We launched with just one sweater."

The collection has expanded since but is very tightly edited: only one or two colours are added to their range of long-fibre Merino jumpers every year. The Andersens' showroom-cum-office-and-shop is close to the harbour, maintaining an all-important link to the sea.
110 Vester Voldgade, 1552
+45 2170 0863
andersen-andersen.com

Meet the maker
⎯
You can still walk into many Copenhagen shops and find ateliers out back. One of the prettiest is Inge Vincent's studio-cum-shop on Jaegersborggade. Visit to browse her hand-moulded wafer-thin porcelain cups, vases and lanterns.
vincents.dk

6

Mads Nørgaard, City Centre
Family values

Mads Nørgaard on Strøget has been updating wardrobe classics ever since its designer became disenchanted with the garish clothing ubiquitous in the mid-1980s. "All the successful brands had logos on them so I had to start producing myself," says Nørgaard. An initial menswear line led to collections for women and children – and a reputation for unfussy, discreet designs.

In the well-stocked shop on the saturated – and at times overwhelming – Strøget you'll also find Scandinavian staples such as Acne and Rains alongside in-house offerings that include a signature ribbed T-shirt that was designed by Jørgen Nørgaard in 1967. The T-shirt has since become part of Designmuseum Danmark's permanent collection.
15 Amagertorv, 1160
+45 3332 0128
madsnorgaard.dk

Homeware
Feather your nest

1

Designer Zoo, Vesterbro
Exotic specimens

This townhouse-cum-workshop and retail and exhibition space was founded in 1999 by Karsten Lauristen as a creative platform for fellow designers. Besides the ever-changing stock of 100 guest artisans ranging across homeware, jewellery and furniture, the space also contains six ateliers.

In one, Lars Rank fashions ceramic lamps; in another Bettina Schori blows psychedelic glass vases. "We have a long tradition of arts and crafts in Denmark and we must make every effort to stick to it," says Lauristen.
137 Vesterbrogade, 1620
+45 3324 9493
dzoo.dk

Disappointing lack of big cats in Designer Zoo...

②
Normann Copenhagen, Østerbro
Internationally renowned

A narrow entrance on the busy thoroughfare of Østerbrogade belies Normann Copenhagen's expansive shop within. A former cinema that closed in 1979, the high-ceilinged space was renovated in 2005 – the same year owners Poul Madsen and Jan Andersen decided their 1999-born design firm was to become a lifestyle shop.

On show is everything from cheerful stationery to colourful chairs and lamps, and clothes by Scandi makers including Libertine Libertine and Acne. Pop-ups from the likes of Copenhagen-based designer Stine Goya (*see page 44*) and special events such as photography exhibitions are commonplace, while upstairs the design team is busy thinking up the brand's versatile accessories and furniture.
70 Osterbrogade, 2100
+45 3555 4459
normann-copenhagen.com

③
Illums Bolighus, City Centre
One-stop design shop

As you may have gathered from the preceding pages, the retail scene in Copenhagen is vibrant and rather vast. Denmark's modern history is peppered with design heavyweights such as Georg Jensen, Børge Mogensen and Finn Juhl, all of whom have paved the way for subsequent generations of prominent designers; this makes navigating the line-up a little daunting.

For an overview of the greats, as well as today's up-and-comers, visit Illums Bolighus on the main pedestrian mall. Since its inauguration in 1925 the department store has lined its shelves with the country's best furniture, homeware and fashion, making it one of the best curations of Danish design in the world.
10 Amagertorv, 1160
+45 3314 1941
illumsbolighus.com

④
Georg Jensen Heritage,
City Centre
Silver service

Denmark's greatest silversmith established his marque in 1904. Jensen's designs blended simple forms with flowing art nouveau motifs that stemmed from his love of nature. Upstairs at the main shop on Strøget you can see some of these original pieces, ranging from wine pitchers and centrepieces to vases and candelabra, alongside the signature styles of the other major designers who have worked for the house over the years. Downstairs there's striking contemporary jewellery, watches and tableware.
4 Amagertorv, 1160
+45 3814 9240
georgjensenheritage.com

Spoilt for choice
—
Stilleben carries stock from 148 makers

Stilleben, City Centre
Prints charming

Ditte Reckweg and Jelena Nordentoft met while studying design and founded Stilleben in 2002. They were among the first Danish shops to sell graphic prints – the cornerstone of their business – alongside ceramics. They believe this mixed offering was the key to their success. The round-up has now expanded to textiles, homeware and furniture from a breadth of designers such as Ilse Crawford and Jesper With. Stilleben's in-house label, a mix of ceramics and stationery, recently introduced its own line of prints.
3 Niels Hemmingsens Gade, 1153
+45 3391 1131
stilleben.dk

Royal Copenhagen

This Copenhagen institution was founded in 1775 and enjoyed royal patronage from the start. In 1790 the Flora Danica set of 1,802 pieces was commissioned as a gift to Catherine the Great from Danish king Christian VII; it took 12 years to complete and is today on show at Rosenborg Castle (and still used for state dinners). You can pick up your own version at the Royal Copenhagen shop on Strøget.

In 2008, production of the trademark blue-and-white porcelain was moved to a factory in Thailand but the 15 Flora Danica artisans remained in Denmark. Training for these rarefied roles is intense, beginning with a supervised four-year period where the apprentice must learn to paint the country's 3,200 indigenous plants that appear in the series. After this, all pupils must undergo a further six years of on-the-job instruction.
royalcopenhagen.com

Paustian, Nordhavn
Winning combinations

The Paustian principles of sourcing original furniture and good design are unchanged since Ole Paustian set up his first shop in Vesterbro in 1964. So good was his eye that the modular sofa designed by Erik Rasmussen in 1969 is still a hot item. Paustian is retired but his spirit lives on in the airy showroom created by celebrated architect Jørn Utzon in 1987. The heritage-listed space is perfect for showing objects in exhibition-style settings, which eschew dedicated brand areas in favour of mixing classics from Artek and Vitra of Cassina with the house range.
2 Kalkbraenderiløbskaj, 2100
+45 3916 6565
paustian.com

⑦
Hay, City Centre
Fresh thinking

Despite its relative youth, Hay is the paradigm of Denmark's new creatives. Rolf and Mette Hay founded the brand in 2002 to create simple, ergonomic furniture with a Danish aesthetic. At its flagship two-storey showroom you'll find collaborative works by Hay's roster of designers, including armchairs by Leif Jorgensen and the pivot mirror from Lex Pott. Also available is the Wrong for Hay range, launched in 2013 with London designer Sebastian Wrong. Look out for totes, textiles and more from the in-house accessories line.
61 Østergade, 1100
+45 4282 0820
hay.dk

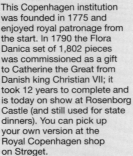

9
Dansk Made for Rooms, Vesterbro
Hand-picked treasures

This pared-down shop near the
hip Meatpacking District is
a treasure trove of homeware,
founded in 2010 by sisters Malene
Sofie and Ma-lou Westendahl.
 Expect Japanese porcelain
by Hasami, Edison bulbs by
Copenhagen favourite Farma,
books and magazines from Cereal
and Bauhaus, and in-house
furniture line Dansk. The selection
in the polished studio never follows
a rigid style; instead every item is
hand-picked informally and on its
own merit by the sisters, creating
a more personable selection.
80 Istedgade, 1650
+45 3218 0255
danskshop.com

⑧
Tortus Copenhagen, City Centre
Potted history

The Danish pottery industry is
kiln-hot and, in the skilful hands of
Eric Landon, it's easy to see why.
"I want to show the world that
you can sit and relax and drink
coffee in a beautiful studio and
then make a pot," says Landon
from his 18th-century workplace in
Copenhagen's old town. This has
been the home of his brand, Tortus
Copenhagen, since 2012.
 Landon (*pictured*) moved to
Denmark from the US in 1999
and has been reviving the country's
centuries-old ceramics scene
ever since. Step inside his studio
and you'll soon see his aesthetic
has a footing in Danish history:
lots of flowing "rabbit fur" glaze,
wabi-sabi imperfections and
streamlined forms.
 Want to get your hands
dirty? Landon also holds hugely
successful workshop courses.
23 Kompagnistraede, 1208
+45 5250 2471
tortus-copenhagen.com

What a dish

Father and son Aage and
Kasper Würtz handmake
fine-dining crockery; the
rough-hewn pieces in speckled
earth tones are used in
restaurants such as Noma,
Fred in Rotterdam and Luksus
in Brooklyn. Head to H Skjalm
P on Nikolaj Plads for a set.
khwurtz.dk

Specialist retailers
Nice and niche

All types
—
More than
200 fonts are
available
here

---

①

Playtype, Vesterbro
Buy the letter

This slender shop furbished
with bold, masculine typefaces
is thought to be the world's
first physical shop selling fonts.
Playtype was opened in 2010 by
Copenhagen-based branding
agency e-Types, which has been
in the font business since 1997.
"We bought the store and started
designing and producing mugs,
posters and notebooks to make it
look like a shop and show off our
different typefaces," says creative
director Rasmus Drucker Ibfelt,
who works in the firm's studio
around the corner. "What started
as a fun way to communicate
a digital product became, almost
coincidentally, a small business
with a lot of potential."

As well as the multitude of
typefaces available to buy, we
recommend the posters printed in
Denmark on Swedish paper.
6 Vaernedamsvej, 1619
+45 6040 6914
playtype.com

②

Antique Toys and Dolls,
City Centre
Childish pleasures

A small window on a quiet side
street near the Nyhavn waterfront
is the only thing that gives away
the location of this antique toyshop.
But if you enter the 17th-century
building you'll find a beguiling
collection of toys, dolls and other
pre-loved curiosities.

Birgit Muusmann and Peter
Gamdrup began their collection 10
years prior to opening the doors
to their shop in 1990. Today they
source and sell an ever-changing
stock of nostalgic treasures, some
dating all the way back to 1780.
20 Store Strandstraede, 1255
+45 3312 6632
antique-toys.dk

*Ah, no
taxi fare.
Can I get
home in
a toy car?*

③
Cykelmageren, Nørrebro
Pedal power

Bicycles are a way of life in
Copenhagen, and Cykelmageren
("bike-maker") provides the
goods. Rasmus Gjesing founded
the company in 1994, repairing
two-wheelers, but soon began
making them himself. All the bicycle
parts are designed by Gjesing and
hand-crafted in a studio north
of Copenhagen; they are then
sandblasted, painted and assembled
in the city. As well as being made
to measure, the bikes come in three
basic models: the gentlemanly
"tourist"; simplified "sport"; and
forward-leaning "race".
57 Store Kongensgade, 1264
+45 3311 1211
cykelmageren.dk

Pedal pedlar

Soren Sögreni has been in
the bike business since 1981.
Every part of the bike – down
to the bell – is assembled by
hand (where possible) and
each bike gets an hour's test
ride before being approved
for sale. Visit the shop on
Sankt Peders Straede.
sogrenibikes.com

④

Blomsterskuret, Frederiksberg
Blooming marvellous

While Martin Reinicke was running his own vintage furniture shop – at the tender age of 23 – he learned that a neighbouring flower shop was coming up for sale. "I saw the possibility of combining the two," he says. Now, a decade later, his squat shop, tangled in greenery and sandwiched between commercial lots along Vaernedamsvej, sees a constant flurry of Copenhagers vying for his latest bouquet featuring rare and peculiar species. "We try to make arrangements that reflect the northern native flora with a twist of anarchy and humour," he says. Reinicke also produces his own pottery collection, and if you're in need of a gift card to accompany one of his handsome bunches of flowers, just pop across the road to Playtype *(see page 55)*.
3A Vaernedamsvej, 1819
+45 3321 6222
blomsterskuret.dk

Lego

Lego began life in the wooden-toy business when carpenter Ole Kirk Kristiansen founded the company in 1932. Derived from the Danish words *leg* (play) and *godt* (well), Lego's plastic brick sets are one of the world's most recognised toys. Manufacturing still takes place in Denmark, as well as factories in Hungary, the Czech Republic and Mexico, plus there's a facility planned in China. The Lego flagship sits on the tourist trap of Vimmelskaftet but is worth the visit to seek out some of the more elusive sets and see the near-complete range from the Architecture series. A day trip to Legoland in Billund is also possible but requires an early start and takes three hours each way by car or train.
lego.com

Furniture
Have a seat

Wood land
——
All wooden pieces are made on the isle of Fyn

①

Carl Hansen & Søn, City Centre
Timeless pieces

Across the two floors of this flagship shop, designer Hans J Wegner's classics abound. While the master's archive keeps yielding designs that are ripe for re-release, Carl Hansen & Søn has two pieces that have been in continuous production for the last half century: the Wishbone chair and the SC25 lounge chair. Some of the weaving work is done in the workshop over the road where live craftsmanship demonstrations take place. One chair, the Faaborg by Kaane Klint, takes up to 20 hours to painstakingly intertwine.
21 Bredgade, 1260
+45 6447 2360
carlhansen.com

The Apartment, Christianshavn
House hunting

The homely concept of this discreet shop is a refreshing counterpoint to Copenhagen's uber-sized – and often repetitive – design retailers.

Tina Seidenfaden Busck founded The Apartment in 2011. She handpicks her inventory of 20th-century furniture and contemporary art and design pieces from Scandinavia and southern Europe. "The aim is to create a more intimate and personal experience," she says. "The environment makes it easy for our clients to see what a piece will look like in their own homes."
33 Overgaden neden Vandet, 1414
+45 3162 0402
theapartment.dk

Wow factor — This space was once a bridal shop

2 By Lassen Concept Store, City Centre
Design greats unearthed

By Lassen's Kubus candleholder is almost as omnipresent in Danish homes as the Wishbone chair. The extensive archive of designs by modernist architects Mogens and Flemming Lassen form the backbone of this collection. It was founded in 2008 by Mogens Lassen's great-granddaughter, who discovered millions of sketches by her ancestor, many of which had never been produced. The company also makes upholstered chairs (including the Tired Man model) and geometric storage.
20 Holbergsgade, 1057
+45 3616 8000
bylassen.com

Broad remit — &Tradition has reissued classics such as Arne Jacobsen and Flemming Lassen's Mayor sofa, as well as commissioning contemporary designers such as Jaime Hayon and Sami Kallio. To view the covetable range, visit their warehouse on Papirøen. *andtradition.com*

④
Gubi, City Centre
French inspiration

Gubi Olsen and his wife Lisbeth founded his product-design company in 1967. Throughout the years the duo found inspiration in Napoléon Bonaparte's legacy, the fancifulness of French cinema and the splendour of grand pianos. Today the company is headed by their son Jacob who, aside from making the signature range, has steered Gubi to reissue peculiar and forgotten furniture and lighting designs from the 20th century. The expansive two-floor showroom is more of an ode to masterful design than a traditional retail space.
19 Møntergade, 1140
+45 5361 6368
gubi.com

⑤
Studio Oliver Gustav, City Centre
Weighty affair

More curator than retailer, Oliver Gustav selects everything based on his own aesthetic: heavy, sculptural objects in raw materials. "When you step into this space it's like stepping into the inner part of myself," he says. The shop feels anti-Scandi, with grey walls, Vincenzo de Cotiis furniture, Apparatus light fittings and monochromatic art. "We try to show things new to Copenhagen or that you can't get anywhere else." He matches costly one-offs with artfully arranged curios, steel-boxed candles or smudgy coloured Society linens made exclusively for him.
9 Store Strandstraede, 1255
+45 2737 4630
olivergustav.com

⑥
Roxy Klassik, Frederiksberg
Top drawer

Vintage emporium Roxy Klassik began selling authentic designer mid-century wares in the early 1980s in this small space along Godthåbsvej. The shop soon doubled its floorspace and a second outpost opened in Nørrebro. In 2005, the company was bought by Thomas Schlosser, who also owns the Klassik flagship in central. But the most extensive range can be found in the rough-around-the-edges warehouse in Amager which feeds all of the shops. The superlative selection of chairs, coffee tables, silverware and more hail from greats such as Mogensen, Wegner and Jensen.
20 Godthåbsvej, 2000
roxyklassik.dk

Can you carry this for me please? I have a spree to complete.

Antique hunting

There are antique shops all over the city. To save crisscrossing the capital, head to the cluster along Ravnsborggade in Nørrebro, just a block back from the lakes. Among them are Veirhanen and LH-Møbler, both with a mid-century bent. The cluttered collections of Antik & Kunst and ABC Antik offer vintage Royal Copenhagen pieces. Brodersen Kunst & Antikvitetshandel specialises in antique books and artwork. An occasional flea market also pops up on selected weekends.
ravnsborggade.dk

⑦
Fredericia, City Centre
Streamlined seating

Despite starting as an upholstery workshop in 1911, Fredericia found its fame from 1955 onwards when collaborations with Denmark's eminent designer Børge Mogensen began, and his Model 201 sofa became a company staple. Its roster of designers has expanded, with contributions from GamFratesi to Jasper Morrison, but Mogensen's creations (including the lauded Spanish and People's chairs) still make up most of the streamlined pieces in this light-filled showroom. The designer's own sketches adorn the stripped-back walls.
22 Frederiksborggade, 1360
+45 3312 4644
fredericia.com

Books and records
Stop, look and listen

❶
Politikens Boghal, City Centre
Bookworm's delight

This bookshop lives up to its catchline: "Matching people with books for more than 100 years". Focusing on Danish literature, it also has a wide selection in English. "Most younger people can read in English and this means the good books are available sooner and cheaper," says manager Christina Thiemer, who cut crime to make room for English classics. She's put in a glass staircase to open up the basement, set sofas in sunny alcoves for browsers, and gives such prominence to poetry you'll wish you could read Danish.
37 Rådhuspladsen, 1785
+45 3067 2806
politikensforlag.dk

Now we just need some books. And a few Mikkeller beers perhaps?

② Sort Kaffe & Vinyl, Vesterbro
Grind and spin

When Christian Rygaard (*pictured, below*) opened his café-cum-record shop in 2006, it was a bold move. "All the record shops were disappearing," he says. He set up in a former artist's studio in the then-seedy Vesterbro, hoping the coffee side of the business would cover any shortfall caused by low record sales – but it was an instant success.

The brimming shelves of records reflect Rygaard's tastes, from Smog and Moon Duo to Thurston Moore and Fela Kuti. "We try to find records that you didn't know you wanted. New artists but also reissues of forgotten masterpieces."
4 Skydebanegade, 1709
+45 6170 3349

books are made, how the paper feels." She also sells prints by Danish illustrators, Japanese packaging and homeware.
9 Landemaerket, 1119
+45 2613 9833
cinnobershop.dk

④ Palermo Hollywood, Nørrebro
Sports and style

Founders Anja Kolby and Cathrine Lundager have avoided the muted minimalism that pervades most retail destinations in town; instead inspiration comes from the sunnier Latin America and southern Italy. Football writer Lundager picks the pared-down shelves of books based on whether she'd want to read them; expect sporting biographies and feminist classics (but magical realist novels also make an appearance). Fashion stylist Kolby selects the other goodies, from jeweller Malene Glintborg's geometric rings to Nørrebro football club jerseys.
31 Jaegersborggade, 2200
+45 2326 6054
palermo-hollywood.com

③ Cinnober, City Centre
Paper view

Across from the 17th-century Round Tower is a design-centric bookshop owned by Ulla Welinder. "I've always loved paper," says Welinder, who opened the shop in 2008 after 20 years pondering what she'd like to sell. "Now I simply choose the products I found useful and inspiring as a graphic designer, or sometimes just because they're beautiful. I also like to consider how

Things we'd buy
—— The city's most coveted

The Danes know a thing or two about good design and while you might not be able to squeeze a Hans Wegner chair or a Finn Juhl sideboard into your suitcase, there are plenty of bite-sized iconic products to take away.

Hygge-up your home with a selection of Menu's minimal homeware and Ditte Fischer's ceramics, or perhaps a Flensted mobile to remind you of this herring-loving country. A pair of sturdy trainers by Legends and a weatherproof jacket by Rains will both combat the city's often inclement climate and keep you looking sharp.

Finally, don't leave without stuffing the pockets of your new mac with the Danes' sweet treat of choice: salt and caramel chocolate-coated Lakrids liquorice, anyone?

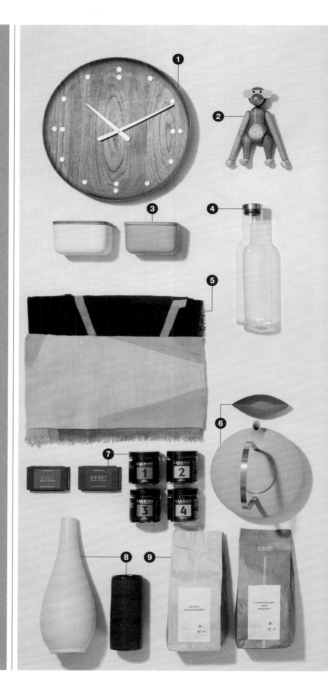

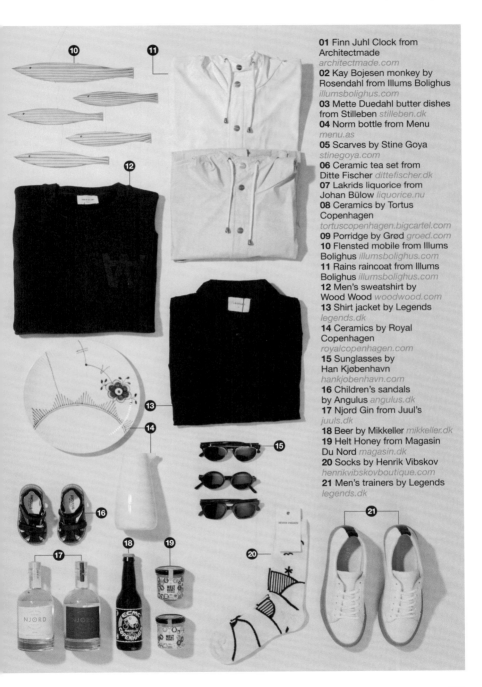

01 Finn Juhl Clock from
Architectmade
architectmade.com
02 Kay Bojesen monkey by
Rosendahl from Illums Bolighus
illumsbolighus.com
03 Mette Duedahl butter dishes
from Stilleben *stilleben.dk*
04 Norm bottle from Menu
menu.as
05 Scarves by Stine Goya
stinegoya.com
06 Ceramic tea set from
Ditte Fischer *dittefischer.dk*
07 Lakrids liquorice from
Johan Bülow *liquorice.nu*
08 Ceramics by Tortus
Copenhagen
tortuscopenhagen.bigcartel.com
09 Porridge by Grød *groed.com*
10 Flensted mobile from Illums
Bolighus *illumsbolighus.com*
11 Rains raincoat from Illums
Bolighus *illumsbolighus.com*
12 Men's sweatshirt by
Wood Wood *woodwood.com*
13 Shirt jacket by Legends
legends.dk
14 Ceramics by Royal
Copenhagen
royalcopenhagen.com
15 Sunglasses by
Han Kjøbenhavn
hankjobenhavn.com
16 Children's sandals
by Angulus *angulus.dk*
17 Njord Gin from Juul's
juuls.dk
18 Beer by Mikkeller *mikkeller.dk*
19 Helt Honey from Magasin
Du Nord *magasin.dk*
20 Socks by Henrik Vibskov
henrikvibskovboutique.com
21 Men's trainers by Legends
legends.dk

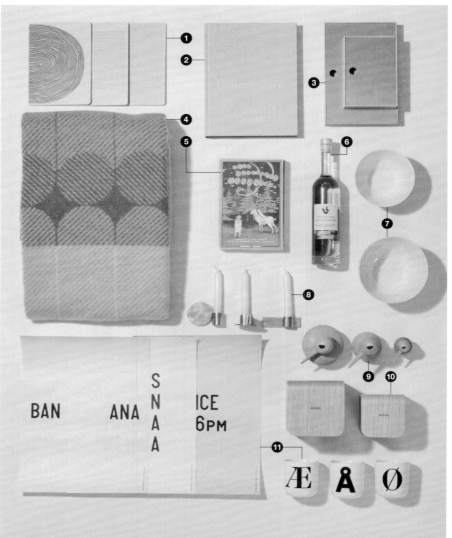

01 Notebooks by Hay
hay.dk
02 Design book from Cinnober
cinnobershop.dk
03 Moebe organisers from
Stilleben
stilleben.dk
04 Blanket by Normann
Copenhagen
normann-copenhagen.com

05 *Hans Christian Andersen Fairy
Tales* from Politikens Boghal
politikensforlag.dk
06 Braunstein Kryddersnaps from
Kjaer & Sommerfeldt *kogs.dk*
07 Mette Duedahl bowls
from Stilleben
stilleben.dk
08 Candle holders from Frama
framacph.com

09 Architectmade birds from
Illums Bolighus
illumsbolighus.com
10 Wood organisers from Illums
Bolighus
illumsbolighus.com
11 Prints and mugs by Playtype
playtype.com

12 essays
──── Copenhagen
chronicles

Hej! Come
and take
a seat, I'll
read you
a story

ESSAY 01

Live and let thrive
Lure of Copenhagen

Its weather is gloomy and its taxes soaring – so how come Copenhagen regularly tops polls for having the best quality of life in the world?

by Michael Booth,
author

What is Copenhagen's secret? Why do its inhabitants regularly vote themselves the happiest people in the world and how has their city managed to top MONOCLE's own Quality of Life index more times than any other?

It has taken me a while to work this out, not least because I think it has taken Copenhagen a while too. When I first moved here around the turn of the century it always seemed to be February, no matter the time of year. Coming from London, the Danish capital was, to me, a dull, cold and rather unwelcoming place. It was closed most of the time and the food was lousy. I might as well have been living in a second-tier Polish city – or Hull.

There was one especially dispiriting morning: I had just received a shocking tax bill in the post, was threatened with physical violence by a driver for turning left on my bike at a junction (one is supposed to dismount at the kerb and escort one's bicycle across the road as if it were an elderly auntie) and then been tutted at for using the pedestrian crossing while the light was red (it didn't matter that there wasn't a car in sight). Did I mention that it was sleeting?

Sundays were a particular chore. Where was everyone? What were they doing? (Answer: either playing handball or watching repeats of *Midsomer Murders*.) In the end, I escaped to Paris but the happiness surveys didn't stop. In fact the claims grew louder for Copenhagen as the best city in which to live. What was going on? The clamour grew so loud that eventually I was persuaded to move back.

I returned to a changed and renewed city. Copenhagen had blossomed spectacularly over the previous decade. These days the

---

**Three reasons for
the high quality of life**

01 **Free education**
No tuition fees and students get monthly support from the state.
02 **52-week parental leave**
Parents can receive up to 32 weeks of monetary support.
03 **Active labour market**
Keeps the employed and unemployed skilled.

mood seems more mid-May than darkest February – even in darkest February. Against all the odds this city has become a global magnet for questing chefs. Every week the streets are brought to life by some festival or other. City Hall has worked wonders on the harbour water (you can swim in it now; some lunatics do, year-round) and the transport network continues to expand. Above all, despite rising house prices, the authorities have tried to keep the city centre family-friendly and – take note, London – battle to maintain affordable housing to keep the demographic mix healthy. True, the tax bill is still ludicrous but you do sometimes get a sense of where the money goes.

"The mood seems more mid-May than darkest February – even in darkest February"

It used to be that the tourist board was happy if Copenhagen got a mention on CNN's weather round-up but these days the city is basking in an unprecedented level of global attention. Television shows such as *The Killing*, architects and artists such as Bjarke Ingels and Olafur Eliasson, and those New Nordic chefs, have all kept Copenhagen in the headlines for years now.

Of course, no one here is kidding themselves that they live in Montpellier or Madrid – the wind still howls and the clouds still glower for much of the year – but the Danes are proving that northerners can still enjoy their public spaces and that their cities can do more than merely function: they can help enable nothing less than collective happiness.

So what *is* the secret? Taxes aside, Copenhagen excels in moderation. It strikes a balance between the competing demands of the contemporary capital and therein lies the key not only to its ineffable liveability but its visitability. So while this is a famously enthusiastic biking city, there is also room for cars; the Danes may be Lutherans at heart but they have a more relaxed approach to booze, porn and partying than their Nordic brethren (there's no state-run alcohol monopoly in Carlsbergland); and, above all, they know when to stop working – usually around midday on Friday.

That's when the crowds gather to soak up the sun on Dronning Louises Bro, the bridge that links the city centre to the more multicultural quarter of Nørrebro across the elegant inner-city lakes. It's become the meeting place for a pre-dinner beer or even an urban picnic – a perfect Instagram moment for this most Instagrammable of cities. — (M)

ABOUT THE WRITER: Michael Booth is MONOCLE's Copenhagen correspondent and the author of the bestselling *The Almost Nearly Perfect People: The Truth About the Nordic Miracle*.

ESSAY 02
That special feeling
Meaning of 'hygge'

It's a word that, if you can unlock its intricacies, reveals much about the Danish mindset. If only it were easier to explain.

*by Lise Ulrich,
writer and photographer*

Watch a Dane explain his or her Christmas traditions to foreigners and you'll likely spot a few worried looks as the storyteller waxes lyrical about the centrepiece of Christmas Eve: the tree adorned with multiple lit candles. "They flicker beautifully on a dark winter evening," the Dane might say enthusiastically, while the international audience ponders the fire hazards of numerous flames on a large semi-dry indoor tree. It's not practical but it sure is *hyggeligt*.

Deciphering the Danish word *hygge* goes a long way to understanding the mindset of the Danes, oft voted the happiest people on Earth. Stronger than "homey" and more emotionally laden than "cosy", *hygge* is as much a state of mind as it is a concept used to describe the ambience of everything from interior decoration to social gatherings. Snuggling up on the couch with tea and snacks to watch Netflix with the family is *hyggeligt*, as is making a pleasant new acquaintance.

"Stronger than 'homey' and more emotionally laden than 'cosy', hygge is a state of mind"

"*Hyggeligt* to meet you," Danes will exclaim in greeting, then later see you off with "Have a *hygge* time!" often causing foreigners to conclude that the word equates to the somewhat tamer "nice". But the meaning of *hygge* runs deeper: it sums up the Danes' tireless aim to feel comfortable, happy and at peace, be it at home or in a restaurant, and our wish that you, dear new acquaintance, will experience the same level of relaxed bliss.

Having a wonderful time with friends at home (or alone, although *hygge* is often associated with socialising in good company) or admiring the pleasant atmosphere of a public space is by no means exclusive to Danes, however patenting the concept is uniquely Danish.

The word actually originates in Norway but was introduced to Denmark in the early 18th century, where it quickly took hold. Famed Danish historian and journalist Erling Bjøl once wrote that *hygge* "became an important part of the way Danes see themselves. *Hygge* came to be thought of as something so distinctively Danish that many to this day are convinced that it can neither be translated, nor found elsewhere." A belief, one can argue, that facilitates the Danes' overall feeling of happiness; we genuinely believe the Danish brand of *hygge* is as good as it gets.

Given the harsh climate and long dark winters of the Scandinavian regions it is logical that Danes of yore were drawn to a word that epitomises feeling safe and content, quickly claiming the available-to-all sparkle of candlelight or an open fireplace as key components. And Danes still revel in subdued lighting and candles both night and day, winter or high summer; don't be surprised to see candles on Copenhagen café tables under a bright July sun. We can think of nothing worse than the glare of fluorescent lights

Three of the city's most 'hyggeligt' places

01 Papirøen
Recline here on a deckchair on a warm summer's day.
02 Tivoli Gardens
Cosy up to a loved one just as the fairy lights are turned on.
03 Bevar's
Settle in and order a hot drink on a cold day.

(perhaps another, more egocentric clue to Danish happiness: most people probably feel they look better under soft lighting).

Consequently the chase for *hygge* has played a large part in determining the look and feel of the Danish design scene. Many of the country's most celebrated interior designers have created furniture that corresponds with, and enhances, Danes' love of indoor *hygge*, all while integrating components from the natural landscapes such as wood, wool and stone. Thus, going inside to escape the raging elements for an evening of *hygge* is not so much about separating oneself from the outside as it is about implementing nature in the home to enjoy in all seasons (think sheepskins casually flung over the cognac-coloured leather back of a wooden armchair). Several now-iconic furniture designs have become all but synonymous with *hygge* – in private homes in Copenhagen it can seem as though flanking the dining room table with Arne Jacobsen's Series 7 chair is akin to a national birthright.

Yet this sidelining of *hygge* with sometimes costly interior design does not distract from the now centuries-old belief that Danish *hygge* is bereft of snobbery, never requires fancy dress and is, above all else, honest (although not too honest: one should not disrupt it with tales of personal woe that may make people uncomfortable). Pretentious environments or people do not facilitate a *hyggelig* time and the thought that *hygge* blooms at opposite ends of rich and poor has been central to the Danish

social philosophies of equality and the making of a well-functioning welfare state. Even the modernist landmark of the Louisiana Museum of Modern Art, north of Copenhagen, is big on *hygge*, as its fireplace warms the café in winter. Similarly at world-famous Noma, four times crowned best restaurant in the world and holder of two Michelin stars, there is no superciliousness or white tablecloth dramatics: guest are treated to an atmosphere that is disarmingly down-to-earth. Unsurprisingly, Noma chef René Redzepi favours Café Det Vide Hus which has unpretentious *hygge* in spades. Want to put your feet up and treat the place as your living room for the afternoon? Go right ahead, as long as you have a *hyggelig* time.

In recent years, however, with health crazes sweeping the nation it has been somewhat ominously suggested that the fundamental culture of *hygge* could be a strong factor as to why so many Danes find it difficult to lay off "forbidden" pleasures such as alcohol and tobacco. *Hygge* is very much about indulging without prejudice; restrictions on personal freedom and lifestyle choices are far from *hyggeligt* and therefore decidedly non-Danish. Striking a balance between healthy living and *hygge* will prove a curious challenge for future generations.

Hygge is not always practical or easily explained. But with Danes reclaiming the top spot in the UN's World Happiness Report of 2016 it seems to equal social contentment even in an increasingly topsy-turvy world. As do those pretty live candles on the Christmas tree. *Hav det hyggeligt!* — (M)

ABOUT THE WRITER: Lise Ulrich is a writer and photographer for the magazine *Oak The Nordic Journal*, a leading biannual publication about Nordic culture, food and design. When not delving into her native Denmark's obsession with all things *hyggeligt*, she seeks to capture the sweet melancholy of the Scandinavian landscapes with her camera.

ESSAY 03
Days of plunder
Denmark's Viking heritage

The era of the Vikings
may be long since past
but the legacy they left to
Danish culture lives on.

*by Kay Xander Mellish,
author*

**Three surprising
facts about the Vikings**
———
01 They had great hygiene
Excavations have uncovered
tweezers, razors and combs.
02 They dyed their hair
Men used lye soap to bleach
their hair and beards blonde.
03 They skied for fun
Skiing was considered efficient
and a recreation.

Some scholars claim that the Viking age ended in the 11th century but I disagree. In Copenhagen I see Vikings every day.

Now that long beards are fashionable it's easy to picture the Danish postman delivering my package in a long tunic, with an animal skin over his shoulder, swinging an axe. I imagine how odd his curly red locks, pink skin and watery blue eyes must have seemed to the Native Americans as he first set his sock-like leather boots on the shores of Newfoundland. And then I sign for my package and he goes away peacefully.

While the Viking era was the last time Scandinavia dominated Europe, many modern Danes like to argue that they're not the true descendants of the Vikings – the real Vikings, they say, left Scandinavia and went to countries such as England and France.

Genetically, however, today's Danes can be linked to those of Viking days and the Vikings and their artefacts are still seen as a hefty part of the national heritage.

They take up most of the prime space in the National Museum of Denmark in Copenhagen and there are even centres in the countryside where you can live like a Viking with your family for a week, eating food such as rough brown bread and venison and experiencing Viking-era plumbing.

Danish children get a good dose of Viking history at school, where they cut out and paint cardboard battle shields, learn how to draw runes and are taught how to plan and cook for an ocean voyage.

Danish sports still reflect Viking heritage too and not just in the silly plastic-horned helmets that fans wear to national football matches (real Vikings never wore horned helmets; in fact, their origins have been traced to a 19th-century costumer of a Wagnerian opera). But seafaring, a key part of the Viking business plan, is still one of Denmark's sporting strengths: along with rowing and canoeing, sailing is one of few Olympic sports in which the country does well.

Of course, all this homage serves to gloss over the less charming tendencies of these barbaric invaders. The red-bearded men of the past collected their wealth through a Dark Ages form of terrorism (in texts from the period, the word "Viking" is used interchangeably with "pirate"), descending on a place and confiscating its assets while hacking off the limbs of men and forcing themselves on women. Slavery was a key part of Viking society, as was human sacrifice. It's hard to imagine that a nice guy like my postman could ever have been involved in such a thing.

That said, some of the admirable things about today's Denmark can be traced back to Viking culture. The Danes' famous social welfare state, for example, probably has its roots in the Viking habit of living not in small private homes but in windowless "longhouses" shaped like upside-down sailing ships.

These structures would shelter entire extended families, along with their slaves, animals and any guests or wanderers who happened to turn up. You needed a lot of co-operation to make it through the pre-global warming Danish winters.

Longhouses also had room for looms and spinning wheels; Denmark has been exporting cloth for more than 1,000 years. Due to the availability of dye and plants, the Vikings wore mostly blue, black, green and grey. Tastes have not changed: you'd be hard pushed to find people wearing any other colour on a Copenhagen street today (unless the national football team is playing in which case red is approved).

"The origins of horned helmets have been traced to a 19th-century costumer of a Wagnerian opera"

As much as the marauders loved stealing gold, they were also pretty good at fashioning it into jewellery: in the national museum you'll see gold belt buckles, cloak pins and arm rings. Wander down the smaller side streets of the city today and you'll find tiny shops filled with their descendants: young goldsmiths selling delicate earrings and rings. So why not make like a Viking and return from your voyage bearing some of that treasure? Just remember: these days, paying for it is the done thing. — (M)

ABOUT THE WRITER: Kay Xander Mellish is the author of *How to Live in Denmark* (2015). She delivers presentations around the country, helping Danes and foreigners live and work together better.

ESSAY 04

Life cycles
Copenhagen bicycle culture

——

If you're planning on spending any time at all in Copenhagen, there's just one thing you'll need – and it has pedals.

by Mikael Colville-Andersen, writer

Understanding life with bicycles in Copenhagen may seem daunting but it really is a simple affair. I moved to the city a couple of decades ago. After a few days I was sitting in my friends' flat and they gave me the lowdown: "If you're going to live here you need to know two things," I was told. "One is that FC Copenhagen is now your preferred football team. The other is that you'll need a bike. Neither of these points are up for discussion."

They tossed a bike key to me. "It's green and it's somewhere in the garden." It took a while but I found it. Squeaky and rusty – but definitely trustworthy. And so I embarked on a bicycle life, never to look back. It was a crash course in what the bicycle means to urban life in this city.

**Three ways to
cycle in style**
—
01 Raincoat from Rains
rains.dk
**02 Han Kjøbenhavn
clip-on sunglasses**
hankjobenhavn.com
**03 Knitted scarf
by Emdal Studio**
emdalstudio.com

Coming to Copenhagen? Well, the rules are simple: find a bicycle, ride it. It won't take long to figure out the details. You'll soon realise that the infrastructure network is directly inspired by the three basic principles of Danish design: practicality, functionality and elegance.

The intuitiveness of the cycle tracks provides a gentle subconscious tailwind, easing your journey from A to B and beyond. The city has published a bike map, which is amusing to those who live here, simply because every street in Copenhagen and, indeed, in the Capital Region, has infrastructure or facilities to keep you safe.

If you get confused, pointers are easy to find. There are several hundred thousand people riding for transport every day – about 63 per cent of the population. If the rookie fish in the school loses its way, it can just look around at what the others are doing and follow suit. That's you in Copenhagen: a fantastic creature in a huge flock, forever surging forward to new destinations.

And there's the rub: it's all about the destination. The bicycle ride is just a detail. I still meet avid cyclists from Captain Spandex's merry band of racers who come here expecting to find their tribe. How disappointed they are to discover that Copenhageners don't do "cycling gear" and that half the bicycles in the city squeak as they roll along. We'll also look confused if asked about recommendations for a nice ride. Just ride wherever you're going – it'll be nice.

We cycle in flip-flops in summer and wear scarves in the chilly winter months. Dress for the season like you would if you were a pedestrian or bus passenger. Dress for your destination, not your journey.

Ah. There it is again: destinations. Get out and see whatever it is you need to see in the city and only consider doing it on a bike. Here for a weekend? You'll cover more ground on two or three wheels than you ever would on foot or by public transport. Here for longer or on business? The bicycle is still the logical, logistical choice. Trying to decide which bar or café to visit? Look for the one with the most bikes parked outside.

Find a bicycle, ride it. Most hotels have bikes for their guests. Many Airbnb hosts will rustle them up too. There are loads of rental shops and, if you want to splash out and buy one, the city has about 600 bike retailers. We also have share bikes but they are quite possibly the stupidest models on the planet and cost more than renting. Plus, you'll stick out like a sore thumb as a tourist so if you like to blend in, avoid them like the plague.

We too would love nothing more than to have you blend in so do us a favour: please don't mess with our flow. We have places to go, things to do and we're Danish about it. You'll soon discover that cycling here is structured. Hoping to pedal along on a bumblebee-like trajectory, whistling Aqua tunes? You might be disappointed. If you want that then head to Amsterdam. It's acceptable to cycle alongside someone and have a chat but stick to the right so that people can overtake. If you hear a bell, yes, it's for you. If learning Danish swearwords is on your bucket list, try cycling on the pavement or the wrong way down a cycle path.

"Avid cyclists come expecting to meet their tribe. But we don't do 'cycling gear' and half the city's bicycles squeak"

Figure out our flow and adapt to it. It's structured but it's beautiful. It's a ballet of human-powered movement if you want to get all New Nordic romantic about it, but it's one that leads to bars, restaurants, museums and all the cool stuff.

It's simple. It's effective. It's lovely. It's Copenhagen. Find a bicycle, ride it. — (M)

ABOUT THE WRITER: Mikael Colville-Andersen is the CEO of Copenhagenize Design Company, a urban-design firm that promotes cycling culture around the world.

ESSAY 05
Illuminating visions
City of light

You can't fully appreciate Copenhagen until you perceive the peculiarities and interplay of its light and shade.

by Jeni Porter, writer

People in Copenhagen are obsessed and inspired by light – or, more to the point, the absence of it. Light influences art, architecture, design and how people live. In the winter months it's about shades of grey or shards of light; in summer the brighter light and long twilight lift the spirit.

Copenhagen-born artist Mika Utzon Popov talks about the city's winter light as it transitions from warm greys to cold greys, how it mirrors the sea or how the heavy sky "comes down and parks itself on the ground" and there's no horizon. Utzon Popov lives in Sydney, where the sunlight is so harsh he feels as if he's at war with or in awe of it. Coming from Sydney to Copenhagen, as I did, it takes time to acclimatise and to appreciate the subtleties of the changing light.

Then one winter's day the sun peeks out from heavy clouds and throws a silvery beam of light you can almost touch – and you understand it.

You get all those bright white walls, whitewashed floors, light timbers and Louis Poulsen light fittings. You get the candles bought in boxes of 30 at the supermarket and lit, sometimes, before lights are turned on. You understand why having a white building across the road from your apartment is considered a boon because of the reflected rays, what Danes call "poor man's sunlight".

You understand the city's clean modern architecture, where the focus is on how light hits the different surfaces. It could be the shadows that the sculptural winter trees throw on the grey marble walls surrounding Arne Jacobsen's Danmarks Nationalbank building (*see page 108*) or the elevated sitting areas that look like folds of granite on the sunny corners of Israels Plads.

You understand why architects consider winter even when they're designing a summer swimming bath. White Arkitekter installed dramatic lighting on the Kastrup Sea Bath so that it might look good during the "long, dark off-season".

"There is an unspoken worship of light because we are so removed from it at certain parts of the year; it becomes a part of how you think on an intuitive level," says designer Peter Bundgaard Rützou, whose practice Space Copenhagen is renowned for capturing a Scandinavian essence in the atmosperic interiors of restaurants such as Noma and Geist. "Sometimes when Nordic light hits it's as if time is suspended or stretched," he says.

"There is an unspoken worship of light because we are so removed from it"

"There's a beauty in it that lures you in."

He could be describing a Vilhelm Hammershøi painting in which the shafts of light are almost viscous. Living in Copenhagen at the turn of the 20th century, Hammershøi painted reality in an ethereal way, repeatedly depicting the same rooms of his home at 30 Strandgade in Christianshavn with fewer and fewer objects until there was just a window and a ray of light – "Sunbeams or Sunshine" as he called his most emblematic painting, in which time does indeed stand still.

You can draw a line from Hammershøi through to modern Nordic architecture's sensitivity to light. Master proponent Henning Larsen treated light as a "fellow player in architecture" arguing that it was light, both natural and artificial, that creates the rooms and the atmosphere, and that everything else flows from there. The Copenhagen Opera House is not his best work but it still shows how by incorporating daylight into concert houses that are largely for night-time use he gave them a focus on life and the present moment.

"Many people simply lack nuances in their language to express the importance of light. I've always wanted to do something about that by showing the light in my houses," he wrote.

And "nuance" seems to be the key word: to stop for a moment and appreciate the subtleties of light and shade around Copenhagen is to become that little bit closer to the thinking of those who live there. — (M)

Contemporary artists who play with light
—
01 Trine Søndergaard
Art photography.
trinesondergaard.com
02 Jeppe Hein
Interactive installations.
jeppehein.net
03 Nicolai Howalt
Conceptual photography.
nicolaihowalt.com

ABOUT THE WRITER: Jeni Porter is a writer and editor. She swapped the bright lights of Sydney for the nuanced Nordic lights of Copenhagen in 2013. A true Copenhagener, she cycles everywhere and downs tools whenever the sun comes out.

ESSAY 06

Diamond in the rough
Cultural melting pot

———

The neighbourhood
of Nørrebro was, until
relatively recently,
a notorious troublespot.
Nowadays it's a showcase
of Copenhagen's vibrant
mix of ethnicities.

*by Nana Hagel,
writer and photographer*

Having lived in Nørrebro my entire grown-up life, what I appreciate most about the neighbourhood is its diversity. With about 75,000 residents spread across just 4 sq km, Nørrebro is not only the smallest neighbourhood in the city but the most densely populated. There are hipsters hanging out in the summer sun on Queen Louise's Bridge; young families with strollers making their way down the narrow pavements of the area's main street; the elderly and retired who have lived their entire lives in the neighbourhood; and Danes of different ethnic origin that – when you're in Nørrebro – are not so different after all. Despite the limited space, Nørrebro has just enough room for everyone to feel at home.

To call it an undiscovered part of the city would be a slight exaggeration. In recent years the arrival of Michelin chefs, fashionable shops and trendy wine bars have helped put Nørrebro firmly on visitors' radars. But it wasn't always so: when I moved into my first apartment on the busy Nørrebrogade about 10 years ago my father gave me a puzzled look as if he couldn't understand why anyone would want to live in such an area. At that time Nørrebro was synonymous with riots, clashes between police and the left-wing youth, mainly concentrated around the notorious and now departed Ungdomshuset, the Youth House at 69 Jagtvej. Although the Youth House users were evicted and the building was razed to the ground in 2007, the area still carries an air of recklessness.

Less polished than Østerbro, less pricey than the city centre and with more open space than Vesterbro, Nørrebro has a welcoming spirit, a rebellious attitude and a lively atmosphere. Visitors regularly make their way to the charming cobblestone streets lined with independent shops, the larger squares with great coffee houses and the restaurants serving world-class food. But there's another side to Nørrebro that makes a visit to grasp the history and essence of the area worthwhile.

**Three special
places in Nørrebro**

01 Stengade 30
Historic indie music venue.
02 Assistens Kirkegård
Leafy cemetery that doubles
as a summer sunbathing spot.
03 Superkilen
Striking public park split into
three distinctive zones.

For instance, the kebab shops in the northern part of the area serve quality shawarma at ridiculously low prices and make for a different dinner experience in the city. Visiting the numerous public parks and open spaces of the area will give you an idea of life in Nørrebro; it's where locals gather with friends and family on Sundays to barbecue, let their kids play or just hang out on blankets. The many secondhand shops tucked away in basements appeal to a fashionable crowd looking for a bargain and mothers shopping for budget-friendly children's clothes and toys.

"Former residents miss the neighbourhoods sense of togetherness"

Nørrebro is also home to a number of community groups that initiate all kinds of events and gatherings. For instance, there's ByOasen (The Urban Oasis), an unorthodox farmhouse in an area known for its nursing homes and care facilities. Children of all ages come here to experience rural life for a few hours; they play with the rabbits, guinea pigs and hens, while the elderly take joy in activities designed to foster meaningful relationships between the two age groups. Another project, Netvaerk På Tvaers (Network Across Cultures), hosts monthly dinner clubs at the local community centre and encourages citizens of all nationalities to meet around cooking and social activities.

Perhaps because of initiatives like these there's a special feeling of community among the people who live in Nørrebro (although, of course, I am biased). But even friends – former residents of Nørrebro now living in other parts of town – agree with this notion. They miss "home", the sense of togetherness that encapsulates the neighbourhood.

Whether you come to Nørrebro for the best cup of coffee in town, a world-class dinner in one of the new and trendy restaurants or to run an errand in one of Nørrebrogade's diverse shops (followed by a quick kebab), you'll be entering a completely different Copenhagen. — (M)

ABOUT THE WRITER: Nana Hagel is a Copenhagen-based writer and photographer covering travel, design and food. Born and bred in Copenhagen, she has lived in Paris and New York but always returns to her home city.

ESSAY 07

Fish and kings
A storied city

———

From Vikings to warlike monarchs and a reputation as Europe's herring hub, Copenhagen's past is colourful to say the least.

by Flemming Emil Hansen, writer

"Copenhagen was a regional powerhouse that controlled much of the trade in the Baltic Sea"

Megalomaniacal monarchs, fierce clergymen, lost battles, failed alliances, devastating fires, plague, cholera and misery. It's a wonder Copenhagen has turned out as well as it has.

Today the city is a prosperous destination littered with funky cafés, sassy bars, gourmet restaurants and Scandinavian design outlets. Its streets are abuzz with bearded hipsters and bicycles, a hip and modern metropolis with a distinct and disarming air of old-world nostalgia.

Nobody sells this more eloquently than Her Heavy Smoking Majesty, Queen Margrethe II, her eternally youthful marathon-running heir Crown Prince Frederik and his Tasmanian-born wife Crown Princess Mary, who (somewhat fittingly) worked in PR before being whisked away by the prince on a white yacht. Indeed, what the monarchy amounts to nowadays is a non-stop branding campaign for Copenhagen and country alike.

It wasn't always like this. The royal house shaped and defined the city for centuries. But regal dynasties aside, the city's power lay with a fish: herring, to be precise. A key commodity in Europe in the second half of the first millennium, herring was the gold of its day and the rich population found in the narrow strait between Copenhagen and Sweden a mere 20km away turned the area into a sort of Nordic Klondike – albeit a smelly one.

But Copenhagen's first settlements date back far further than that, to around the start of the Viking era, 800 to 1050. The Vikings, to be fair, were proficient in more than just pillaging: they were skilled seafarers, farmers, craftsmen, merchants and fishermen. By the time the last Viking ditched Odin and Thor in favour of Jesus the initial settlements had grown into a regular town and trading station.

In 1160 King Valdemar the Great decided to sign Copenhagen over to Absalon, who was the bishop of Roskilde, the archbishop of Lund, Valdemar's own foster-brother and the country's most powerful clergyman. Absalon had studied theology in France but was as prone to consult the sword as he was the Bible. Copenhagen was awarded to him as a kickback for his loyal support in the bloody feud that united the Danish realm under one throne in 1157. Until then the country had been split into three kingdoms: Valdemar reigned over Jutland and King Knud V over the islands, while King Svend Grathe ruled the county of Skåne. King Svend, however, had Knud murdered at the "Bloodfeast in Roskilde", a *Game of Thrones* style reconciliation party from which Valdemar only narrowly escaped, wounded and set on revenge. Absalon helped Valdemar rally the back-up required to confront Svend on the battlefield and the feud concluded in a big shebang at Grathe Heath in Jutland, where Svend was defeated, captured and killed by the blow of an axe.

Those were the glorious days of flying daggers, swooning maidens and blood-drenched heroes – and Absalon, the holy man, was known to keep up with the best. In the first chronicle of Denmark's early history, *Gesta Danorum* (*Deeds of the Danes)*, its author, Saxo Grammaticus, describes in one chapter how Absalon led a small band of men in battle against 20 ships of Vendian pirates. The pirates were defeated and decapitated, their heads mounted on spikes outside Copenhagen as a warning to others that the archbishop meant business.

Gesta Danorum (which dates from around 1200) was commissioned by Absalon himself and contains the first reference to the name "Copenhagen". Grammaticus notes that Absalon started building a fortified castle in 1167 in "Portus Mercatorum" (Merchants Port), which in turn translates to Købmaendenes Havn. Its short form is København: the Danish name for Copenhagen.

Absalon made Copenhagen a regional powerhouse that controlled much of the trade in the Baltic Sea region and waged wars against competitors and foes. It remained under church rule until 1420, when King Eric VII picked it as new capital of the so-called Kalmar Union, which his adoptive mother Queen Margrethe I had formed by uniting Denmark, Norway and Sweden under one crown. The initial ramparts were soon pushed back to make room for new neighbourhoods and housing for labourers and seamen – the city began taking shape.

More than anyone it was Christian IV, a war-thirsty and flamboyant monarch, who helped lay the foundation of modern Copenhagen. He ruled from 1588 to 1648 and erected many of the notable buildings that still crown the old parts of Copenhagen today. He also created Denmark's first army and sizeable fleet, and led the country through a number of ill-conceived wars with its neighbours, shedding a huge chunk of its territories and laying waste to the economy along the way. But at least Christian fought with style, most famously against the Swedes at the naval battle of Kolberger Heide. There he took 13 pieces of shrapnel and lost his right eye but still got back up and urged his men on, clinging to the mast of his ship to the end.

He was a hard act to follow but his successor Frederick III took an honest stab at it, losing the Danish regions Halland, Skåne and Blekinge to Sweden. Overall, Danish kings have fared better in peace than in war. In 1807 the British shelled Copenhagen to rubble and made off with the entire fleet because of the king's unfortunate neutrality alliance with Napoleon. And eventually, in 1814, Norway too was lost to Sweden, placing Copenhagen on the outskirts of a minimised kingdom.

Come 1849 King Frederik VII would concede the biggest prize of them all: the power to rule. Winds of political upheaval were sweeping across Europe in those years and when they reached Copenhagen in 1848, 15,000 citizens took to the streets to demand reforms, marching on the royal palace. By the time they arrived, however, the king had already thrown in the towel. The 39-year-old monarch didn't really feel that strongly about ruling anyway, it was said. Thus ended 1,000 years of monarchic rule, peacefully and, quite frankly, as somewhat of a royal bore.

Three historical events that shaped the city
———

01 Copenhagen Fire of 1728
A fire destroys more than a quarter of the medieval city.

02 German occupation
A collaborationist government rules from 1940 to 1945.

03 Øresund Bridge
A road and rail link to Malmö opens in 2000.

With few exceptions, the Danish monarchs have since been window-dressing. Queen Margrethe's grandfather, King Christian X, was one such exception. During the Second World War his solitary daily rides through the streets of German-occupied Copenhagen made him a unifying symbol of stoic, quiet resistance. He may well be one reason that the royal house is as popular today as ever.

Another is the drama-free transition to democracy, which many have ascribed to the amicable and consensus-seeking nature of Copenhageners. It's a stretch but not entirely untrue. Copenhageners are expert yet civilised complainers who will go far to avoid confrontation. Nothing seems too insignificant to justify a round of collective moaning but don't mistake it for discomfort or aggression. Overhear a group of Copenhageners moan about moaners – or moan about moaners that moan about other moaners – and you can safely assume that they're as comfortable, chirpy and pleased as a cat with a freebie coupon for a sushi joint. They're merely synchronising their distastes to reconfirm the group's homogeneity – a key lesson to be learned for sociable visitors to the city.

Copenhageners have a conformable and easygoing approach to urban life: if something is out of whack, they complain, rejoice, shrug it off and move on with things. If you aim to make friends for life you'd be well served to work on your moaning and sharpen your sense of sarcasm before you dive in. — (M)

ABOUT THE WRITER: Flemming Emil Hansen is a Vienna-based Danish freelance journalist who lived in Copenhagen for many years, where he headed up the capital's *Wall Street Journal* office.

ESSAY 08
Danish food unwrapped
Copenhagen cuisine

The New Nordic Food Manifesto revolutionised cooking in Copenhagen and beyond. Now chefs are sharing their knowledge to push the culinary boundaries – and themselves – even further.

by Kristian Baumann, chef

I grew up as the middle child of three in a small town 30km from Copenhagen. As a kid I didn't know I wanted to be a chef but I was in an environment that taught me the values of good food.

During summer my parents would take me and my siblings to pick blackcurrants and redcurrants from the bushes of our garden, as well as thyme and nasturtiums. I remember my mum in the kitchen making elderflower syrup, which she still makes to this day. Even from my school days I have a vivid memory of my teacher walking us into the forest to hunt for mushrooms. I can still recall the smell of the mushrooms sautéing with a simple seasoning of salt.

I fondly remember days spent at Danish-Korean gatherings. My parents adopted me and my older sister from South Korea and they ensured that we remained connected to our heritage. At these gatherings we would sing songs, eat Korean dishes and learn about the country we were from. We would go from eating kimchee to visiting my grandma, who would cook us a pot roast with boiled potatoes and gravy. Looking back now I realise how much of an influence these experiences had on the way I cook, how I think as a chef and how I create dishes. It was such a natural part of life and while it wasn't the same as, say, an Italian mamma, this connection to nature and the passing on of tradition was something that my Danish colleagues and I seemed to share.

For several decades now, Copenhagen and the whole of Denmark have had many great restaurants but they were mainly Italian and French-inspired. I began my career peeling potatoes and picking parsley at a small inn in Farum, which served traditional French food. In the 1990s Claus Meyer was travelling the world and investigating what other countries did with their food culture. Fast forward to 2004 and Claus and René Redzepi along with four others introduced the New Nordic Food Manifesto. The movement revolutionised Danish cooking. René put Copenhagen on the map and gave a guideline to Danish chefs while also encouraging individuality. He paved the way for younger chefs to open their own kitchens based on the values of purity, seasonality, ethics, sustainability and quality.

"I began my career peeling potatoes and picking parsley at a small inn"

If I had to pinpoint the moment that changed the way I look at Danish cooking it would be my first meal at Noma. In Denmark we have a traditional dessert called *aebleskiver* (pancake puffs) made from a batter and normally eaten at Christmas with powdered sugar, and jam made over the summer. But René served one with pork and vinegar powder. It was perfect. This small *aebleskiver* changed my life. René has that influence on people. He and a lot of other chefs based in the city are not only cooking incredible food but pushing to make the world a better place.

When René and I sat down over a coffee to devise a plan for new restaurant 108, we talked

Unexpected ingredients at 108

01 **Wild rosehip petals**
Used to make rose caramel.
02 **Wasabina leaves**
Sourced from Aarstiderne's farm in Humlebaek.
03 **Leftover sourdough bread**
Fermented into a bread miso.

about how we wanted to create something fun. From farm to table, I considered every little detail, even what do I do with the leftover bread? Why not make sourdough cones for ice cream? This is just one of the reasons why it is important to call 108 a Copenhagen kitchen, because it's a kitchen that is open-minded while still respecting the restaurants and recipes that came before – and those that are yet to come. It's a timeless approach to collaboration.

In Denmark we tend to prioritise sustainability; yes it's a small step but it helps the bigger picture and inspires others to make change. The New Nordic Food Manifesto isn't a movement that's going to end anytime soon; I see it thriving for decades to come. Its success lies in the willingness to share knowledge and implement change in our daily lives. From my mum teaching me the recipe for elderflower syrup to restaurants across the city helping each other to improve, the gift of knowledge is invaluable. The most important thing is that we don't hold on to what we know but instead share it in order to grow as chefs and as humans. — (M)

ESSAY 09
Gloom with a view
Nordic noir
———
Copenhagen isn't all sweetness and light. Behind the sky-high happiness levels the clouds are a much darker shade and on TV this beautiful city turns into a an entirely different beast.

by Chloë Ashby, Monocle

Cobbled streets lined with colourful houses, harbour baths so clean you can swim in them, parks blooming with rhododendrons and roses: Copenhagen is a beautiful and bountiful place to live. The quality of life comes at a price – taxes are astronomical and the cost of living is no walk in one of said parks – and then there are those harsh, dark winter months. Still blinded by the city's sunny side? You clearly haven't dabbled in Nordic noir.

Part political thriller, part domestic drama and part police procedural, Nordic noir tells twisted tales in bleak urban settings. It has its roots in Danish TV dramas such as *The Killing*, *Borgen* and *The Bridge*, each of which takes Copenhagen as its backdrop and features complex characters beaten down by life and work. These are gritty stories that scrape away the public face of life in the Danish capital to reveal its dark underside, stewing with hypocrisy and corruption. Of course, all of the above is bound up with bad weather: persistent

ABOUT THE WRITER: After working at Noma and then helping Christian Puglisi open Relae and Manfreds, the South Korean-born Danish chef founded his first restaurant, 108, in 2016.

drizzle and near-constant cold add to an unpleasant atmosphere and sense of isolation.

Nordic noir questions both the way outsiders see Denmark and the way Danes see themselves. Instead of the always-cosy city with a perfect democracy and citizens who enjoy a happy work-life balance, we confront a city that's raw and – mysterious murders aside – real. The protagonist in *The Killing*, detective chief inspector Sarah Lund (enter Sofie Gråbøl), is forever unsmiling, career-oriented and, let's face it, emotionally stunted. *Borgen* takes Danish politics as its subject, revealing a treacherous political dynamic beneath an egalitarian surface. And in *The Bridge*, Copenhagen (and its co-star: Malmö, Sweden) has to face the usual urban complaints: poverty, drugs and mental illness.

The Danish capital is a vivid backdrop: in *The Killing* the crime is investigated by Lund et al at Politigården, the city's neoclassical police HQ; *Borgen* centres on the home of the Danish government, Christiansborg Palace; and the storyline of *The Bridge* yo-yos back and forth between Copenhagen and Malmö across the 16km-long Øresund Bridge. Everywhere the lighting is moody and grey. "That's what Copenhagen looks like in November," says Piv Bernth, head of drama at DR, the public-service broadcaster that created *The Killing*, *Borgen* and *The Bridge*.

"Copenhagen as we know it disintegrates in these shows. That's part of the charm"

Nordic noir also gives us the everyday. DR is subsidised by the government (ie the Danish tax payer) and therefore has to engage a Danish audience. In Bernth's view this is what has led to the success of these shows abroad. Her motto? "The more local, the more global." What she means is that if you write about what's in front you, what you know, you're more likely to convince your audience. Never is this more crucial than in a crime series: it's the mundane details that make the action plausible rather than absurd. Nordic noir sheds a drastically different

CPH settings in Nordic noir

01 City hall, Central
Centre of Troels Hartmann's campaign in 'The Killing'.
02 Christiansborg Palace
Where political shenanigans play out in 'Borgen'.
03 Øresund Bridge
Links Copenhagen and Malmö in 'The Bridge'.

light on the Danish capital – or rather, extinguishes the light. Although the action unfolds in and around a handful of the city's familiar landmarks Copenhagen as we know it disintegrates in these shows. That's part of the charm. Granted, we see a chic cyclist or two along the way and catch glimpses of fine examples of Danish design – an Arne Jacobsen chair here, a Fritz Hansen coat stand there – but we also bear witness to peripheral spaces, sombre alleyways that hint at sinister goings-on.

"Suddenly we showed this dark and gloomy side to Danish society and that made viewers all over the world curious," says Bernth. And she's right: international audiences were drawn to the dark. Weren't you relieved to find blotches in Copenhagen's minimalist homes? Didn't it make you feel better when you discovered dubious characters among the city's perfect-looking people? The appeal of Nordic noir? It shows that this region – and in this particular case, Copenhagen – is as dysfunctional as everywhere else.

Nordic noir looks past Tivoli Gardens, Hans Christian Andersen and Danish pastries. But do take the grit, the gloom and the danger with a pinch of salt. Copenhagen may be flawed but it's also, let's be honest, rather nice. — (M)

ABOUT THE WRITER: Chloë Ashby, senior sub editor at MONOCLE, has written for the *New York Observer* and *The Guardian*. As Culture editor of this guide she enjoyed exploring the city's museums and theatres – and, nightmares aside, she's now a firm fan of Nordic noir.

ESSAY 10

Design of the times
Danish Modern

In the 1950s Danish Modern furniture took the world by storm. Jeppe Mühlhausen writes of his love for this golden era of design and how it inspired him to create a "living museum" dedicated to it.

by Jeppe Mühlhausen, design expert

My interest in Danish art and design came from my grandfather, who was a painter and the head of exhibitions at Louisiana Museum of Modern Art (*see page 93*) for 10 years from 1959. As a kid I would spend holidays there and he introduced me to that whole world.

I still remember the day my parents bought their first piece of designer furniture – a six-seater Børge Mogensen sofa. It was really, really fine – perfect for napping on. They also purchased a Piet Hein Superellipse table, a lamp by PH (Poul Henningsen) and eight Arne Jacobsen Series 7 chairs.

In the 1970s, our house was somewhat avant-garde, and I was always embarrassed when my school friends would come over. We didn't have carpet, which was pretty out there for the time, and we were one of the last families to get a colour television. My father was a hippie communist – he had a beard down to his chest and wore a Soviet jacket – and my mother smoked a pipe, so you can just imagine.

Like many people, my parents had realised that Danish design could give their home some personality. Danish designers were ahead of their time by recognising this global desire to express status and lifestyle – individuality – through home furnishings. When I moved out of home at 21, I bought my own first pieces of furniture – a PH lamp, a Superellipse table and an Arne Jacobsen chair. I copied my parents' style, basically.

My career led me into hospitality and I became the general manager at Hotel Alexandra (*see page 21*) in 1992, at the age of 29. At the time, the building was very run down and would close for three months during the winter, so I was asked by the board to find a new way to run it.

The hotel had a few pieces of furniture made by Kaare Klint. Klint is often called the father of modern Danish design; he founded the furniture school at the Royal Danish Academy of Fine Arts in 1924 and taught some of the country's finest designers including Børge Mogensen, Hans J Wegner, Nanna Ditzel and Ole Wanscher. He believed that Denmark's heritage of quality workmanship should be both preserved and adapted to new needs.

Klint felt that it was the architect's responsibility to bring order to chaos, and despised anything that didn't serve a purpose. It was an opinion that greatly influenced the following generations, both directly and indirectly. Even though many people took exception to the traditional forms in his designs, it is still his influence that marks the quality and homogeny of Danish furniture design.

The furniture designed in the frugal, postwar 1950s reflected the modesty of the times through their sharp, clean lines and simplicity. It was during these years that Arne Jacobsen created his most famous chairs and buildings. The style of Danish Design was also influenced by the long Nordic winters: people spend so much time indoors that Scandinavian designers have learnt to create environments that are comfortable, uncluttered and practical.

It was Klint's pieces in the old hotel that inspired me to create a design museum that people could stay in. The board accepted my proposal and we slowly began restorations in 1994.

When we started collecting for the hotel we had a lot of help from the Royal Danish Academy of Fine Arts about how we should treat it, and the stories behind each piece. We became passionate about it. Now I train all our staff in design history so they are knowledgable, and understand its historical and cultural importance to Copenhagen.

Originally we bought from auction houses but now many sellers contact us directly because they've heard about the concept of Hotel Alexandra. A couple of times I have found Jacobsen chairs that have been thrown away in the recycling centre in Copenhagen, which is pretty wild.

"We don't worry about guests damaging the furniture; it is so robust and of such high quality"

When we first began collecting we didn't really think about the value of the furniture, it was just so beautiful. But in the past ten years or so, the prices have gone through the roof. We have an extra set of Finn Juhl furniture that we want to sell in order to buy something from a less well-known designer. We had bought it for DKK15,000 (€2,000) but it was valued recently at DKK180,000 (€24,000), it's totally crazy.

We are not worried about the guests damaging the furniture; it is so robust and of such high quality. When people check in we always welcome them with a short story about what's in their room so that they are aware and value it.

Five or six years ago, when we weren't so good at communicating what we were doing, we had a lot of foreign guests who

> **Three iconic pieces at Hotel Alexandra**
>
> **01 Finn Juhl Poet sofa (1941)** A couch with a surrealist touch.
> **02 Nanna Ditzel Ring chair (1958):** This curvaceous seat is also called the 'sausage chair'.
> **03 Verner Panton Ball lamp (1970):** The rebel designer created this lamp from plastic balls.

would stay with us and say, 'Why don't you get rid of all that old furniture?' But now the majority of people come here because they have an interest in it.

My favourite room is the Finn Juhl Room. Juhl was one of the more experimental designers. He was spiritual in his expression: he did not consider a chair simply a product in a room, 'It is a design and a room in itself', he once wrote.

His Poet sofa from 1941 is so beautiful and it has a special significance for me because my father was a lighting technician on Danish national television and the name came from a movie that the sofa was used in, and my dad worked on, called *The Poet and the Little Mother.*

My work is my passion and I am so lucky I can spend my days sharing stories about these designers. And on days off when I visit my mother, I still nap on that old Mogensen sofa. My mum will say, 'You need a rest, go to the couch'. — (M)

ABOUT THE WRITER: Jeppe Mühlhausen is the general manager of Hotel Alexandra in Copenhagen, a 61-room guesthouse dedicated to masterpieces of Danish Modern design.

ESSAY 11
Cultural quirks
Deciphering the Danes

———

Spend a little time in Copenhagen and you're sure to be won over by the charming locals, although they certainly do things a little differently. Here are some points to help lessen the cultural divide.

*by Amy Richardson,
Monocle*

1. They're a trusting bunch

Danes have a beautiful capital city, access to excellent "free" education and healthcare, lots of herrings to put on rye bread and another asset in spades: trust. You'll struggle to find an armed guard in a bank but could quite literally stumble across a pram (with infant inside) left out on a pavement: if so, don't be alarmed, the mother will be inside the shop, merrily trying on clothes, comfortable in the belief that her child is safe and even benefiting from a little airing out.

According to Aarhus University professor Gert Tinggaard Svendsen, who wrote a book on the subject in 2014, called – rather imaginatively – *Trust*, the Danes' capacity for

"It will blow a smoke ring every time a tonne of carbon dioxide is released"

placing faith in their fellow neighbours is a major contributor to their enviable wealth and happiness.

They even believe what their politicians say, which means there are low levels of bureaucratic red tape and, quite simply, shit gets done. Money normally spent on security surveillance and monitoring tax dodgers and welfare scammers can be put towards other things, such as roads and healthcare. It also means the government is more able to greenlight progressive, humanist policies that may hurt the average man's hip pocket, but pay dividends in terms of making people feel secure about the future – an essential ingredient to wellbeing.

It does help that Danes are partial to following the rules (just try crossing the road without the assistance of the green man, you'll feel the eyes burning a hole in your back) and there are low levels of institutional corruption. It is believed

---

Two more quirky facts about Copenhagen
———
01 Freetown Christiana
This autonomous community in Christianshavn has its own flag and currency.
02 Their royal family is Europe's oldest
It dates back to 10th-century Viking kings Harald Bluetooth and Gorm the Old.

that this legacy of upstanding civil service dates back to the 1660s when King Frederik III gave jobs to those who had skills – rather than fancy titles and family connections – and introduced harsh penalties for abuses of power.

2. They want people (including you) to have a good time

In 2009, the city council published "A Metropolis for People": a mission statement for Copenhagen becoming the most liveable city in the world. The manifesto is based on the studies and philosophies of homegrown urbanist Jan Gehl (*see page 87*) and underscores the importance of appealing public spaces for people to relax and socialise in (a laidback approach to public drinking certainly helps in regards to the latter). The council has also stated that it's essential for the health and happiness of every citizen to live within a 15-minute walk of a body of water or a green space. Visitors benefit from this too, of course: on a warm day, just head to any park or stretch of boardwalk and soak up the *hygge*.

3. They have a history of looking out for each other

When the Nazis occupied Copenhagen, more than 7,000 Danish Jews fled to Sweden to wait out the war. When these families returned years later, many found that their rents and mortgages had been paid for the duration of their absence, the neighbours had been feeding their pets, and their jobs and businesses were waiting. In some cases, where a home had been re-let, possessions had been inventorised, packed up and put into storage for safekeeping. That the Ministry of Foreign Affairs of Denmark was able to negotiate with the Gestapo in order to protect Jewish assets must surely be one of the more surprising diplomatic achievements during those dark years.

4. They love a grand public statement (especially about the environment)

Copenhagen has another lofty goal: to become the world's first carbon-neutral capital by 2025. So the city has been busy building kilometres of cycle tracks and hectares of wind farms, fitting street lights with energy-efficient bulbs, and so on. But the most striking manifestation of this ambition is the new Amager energy plant, due for completion in 2017. Aside from turning more than 400,000 tonnes of waste into electricity and heat each year, the building's roof will double as a 31,000 sq m ski slope during winter. Oh and it will blow a smoke ring out of its chimney every time a tonne of carbon dioxide is released, sort of like a giant reminder for residents to put their recycling out. — (M)

ABOUT THE WRITER: **Amy Richardson** is the associate editor for MONOCLE's book series. As editor of this guide, she spent part of a gloriously sunny summer cycling around Copenhagen familiarising herself with the city and it's oft-times baffling – but always endearing – inhabitants.

ESSAY 12
Space odyssey
City living

———

Good architecture is about more than just good buildings: the real improvements to urban living come in the spaces in between. Making those improvements is a lifelong mission.

*by Jan Gehl
architect*

I was born in a provincial town but when I was 18 months old my parents moved to Copenhagen, which was occupied by the Germans. After the war the city, like many other places, was quite poor. There was a great housing shortage and most people used bicycles to get around. But then in the late 1950s the cars came.

People became absolutely hysterical about these motor vehicles. Everything was done to make room for them, to make the cars happy. Every street was filled with traffic and every square was filled with parking spaces. There was even a plan to get the remaining cyclists off the streets. But then the oil crisis of the early 1970s hit and we started to have car-free Sundays to save on oil. It was then that people began

to realise that cycling should be promoted.

I graduated from architecture school in 1960 and was supposed to go out and do all these wonderful things as dictated by the modernists: create high buildings and make sure everybody had sunshine and a view of some grass. But there was not much concern for the spaces between the buildings.

But then I married a psychologist and suddenly I was asked questions such as, "Why are architects not interested in people?" I realised that there was a line between the fields of social sciences, urban planning and architecture that was completely uncovered. The ideology at the time was that you should quickly build lots of affordable social housing in concrete out in the suburbs, row after row after row. But the architects didn't know anything about the impact that their projects were having on those who lived in them. My wife and I were incensed that people were being treated in such a way. So we spent the next 50 years investigating these issues. And because we did this in a Copenhagen university, what we learnt had a profound influence on planning in the city.

In the 1960s there was a strong debate in Copenhagen about how the quality of the built environment influences the social life of a city. My wife and I were celebrated as experts on this but we didn't know everything. We decided that we must find out more about what makes a good city and so we went to Italy for six months to study the piazzas and how they were used. We chose Italy because the tradition was there, the weather was good and there were a lot of people to watch.

It was in 1962 that the main street of Copenhagen [Strøget] was turned into a pedestrian-only thoroughfare. Whether it would work was disputed; we were not like

"In Dallas they put up buildings and then look out of the window to see what's happened"

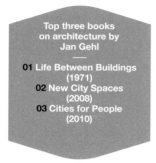

Top three books
on architecture by
Jan Gehl
—
01 Life Between Buildings
(1971)
02 New City Spaces
(2008)
03 Cities for People
(2010)

Italians and it was thought that the climate would never allow for people to be outside. But the moment we reclaimed the space from cars we started to behave like Italians and there was a rapid increase in the life in the city centre.

In 1966 I studied the result of these changes and, after a while, the city became very interested in our work about how Copenhagen could be improved. It was the first time anywhere in the world that systematic research was conducted about how people used a city – most other places study a city's traffic, not its citizens.

Some of the things I have been involved in have roots in Danish culture: the welfare society, the interest in detail and design, the humanistic undercurrent. In Copenhagen it all began with a concern for increasing foot traffic in the shopping areas but quickly became as much about people using the city for recreation time and cultural events. The city invited people to come out of their homes and use its public spaces to cycle and walk – but primarily to have fun, meet their fellow citizens and see what was going on. It is very important for social inclusion – and for democracy – that people partake in public life even if it means sitting quietly on a bench.

Today anyone who wants to put up a new building will be asked very carefully by the city architect, "What does your building do for public life in the city?" It's very different to Dubai or Dallas, where they put up buildings and then look out of the windows to see what's happened.

In many ways my career has been the story of the ugly duckling. For years my colleagues in the university thought I was wasting everybody's time with these studies. But that has changed radically in the past 20 years, particularly after we started our company and actually used the methods and tools we had developed to improve cities such as New York, Moscow, London and Sydney.

Now everybody understands that good architecture is not just about form. If life doesn't like your architecture then it's not good architecture. It could be that it's good sculpture but it's not good architecture unless life is nicely accommodated.

Today it's safe to bike from one end of Copenhagen to the other, even if you're very young or very old. On an ordinary day about 37 per cent of people going to work or studying in the city will arrive on their bikes. On our 45th wedding anniversary, when my wife and I were about 70 years old, we rode into town to have dinner and cycled more than 20km. That could not have happened when we were first married.

We have had the fortune over all these years to wake up together each morning and know that the city is a little bit better than it was yesterday. And that's a wonderful feeling. — (M)

ABOUT THE WRITER: Jan Gehl is an urban-planning expert and the founding partner of Gehl Architects, a consultancy that has helped more than 70 cities around the world increase their liveability through better design.

Culture
—— Sights and
sounds

The compact Danish
capital is chock-a-block
with cultural offerings
that encourage dalliances
with art, music, film
and dance. On rainy days
there are indoor options
aplenty. You'll find a
clutch of contemporary-
art galleries on and
around Bredgade in
the city centre and a
scattering of world-class
museums that stretch
further afield. Often
wrapping around central
courtyards – in one case
a winter garden that
blooms all year round –
these art institutions invite
visitors to experience
everything from
neoclassical sculpture
to Danish design.

All this – along with
old-school cinemas,
live-music venues and
so-called culture houses
– makes for a healthy
dose of the arts. And if
you have a day or two
to spare, popping to a
couple of places out of
town won't go amiss.

Museums and galleries
Painting the town

①
Thorvaldsens Museum, City Centre
Sculpted history

The Thorvaldsens Museum stands
out in today's Copenhagen: the
burnt-orange building looks as it
did when it was built in 1848 as
Denmark's first public museum.
Its purpose? To house the life's
work of Danish sculptor Bertel
Thorvaldsen (1770-1844), who
studied in Copenhagen before
travelling to Rome – and finding
fame – in 1797.

The frieze that wraps around
the two-storey museum shows
Thorvaldsen's welcome-home
reception in 1838 and the sculpture
of Victory on the roof symbolises
what he achieved. Inside are
neoclassical sculptures, as well as
sketches and objects from antiquity.
As you admire the bronze and
marble figures remember to look
up and down: equally impressive
are the starry ceiling and mosaics
beneath your feet.
2 Bertel Thorvaldsens Plads, 1213
+45 3332 1532
thorvaldsensmuseum.dk

Country retreat
——
Frilandsmuseet hosts more
than 80 rural structures that
were built between 1650 and
1940. They were moved here
from their original locations
across Denmark, Germany and
Sweden to give an impression
of centuries-old country life.
natmus.dk/museerne/
frilandsmuseet

Branching out
—
Kunsthal
Charlottenborg
hosts all sorts
of events

(2)

Kunsthal Charlottenborg, Nyhavn
Thought-provoking exhibits

Copenhagen's Botanical Gardens used to sit in the grounds where Kunsthal Charlottenborg now stands: this ivy-laden red-brick structure just off the busy canal-side of Nyhavn was built by architects Ferdinand Meldahl and Albert Jensen in 1883. Created as an extension of the Royal Academy of Fine Arts, which sits just across its quiet courtyard, the exhibition hall was born to host its salons and annual member shows.

Despite going independent between 2007 and 2012, the museum now plays host to the students' graduation shows once more. The programme also includes major contemporary-art exhibitions and retrospectives, as well as concerts and film screenings, all of which take place across an expansive and wide-windowed upper floor.

2 Nyhavn, 1051
+45 3374 4639
charlottenborg.dk

Hmmm, I spy a pretty place to perch

③

Overgaden, Christianshavn
Mixed media

This not-for-profit contemporary-
art gallery has been housed in
a former 19th-century printing
press in a prime position on
the Christianshavn canal since
1986. The works on show vary
in media, with the spacious rooms
particularly lending themselves to
displays of audio and installation
art (a past example being a
retrospective on pioneering lighting
artist Thorbjørn Lausten). The
annual schedule of exhibitions
is supplemented by workshops,
lectures and debates on topics
such as "The Nature of Myth".
17 Overgaden Neden Vandet, 1414
+45 3257 7273
overgaden.org

Pipe dreams
————

This Hirschsprung Collection,
which opened in central
Østre Abkaeg park in 1911,
invites enthusiasts to enjoy
Copenhagen tobacco
manufacturer Heinrich
Hirschsprung's personal
collection of 19th and early
20th-century Danish art.
hirschsprung.dk

Four more

01 National Museum of
Denmark, City Centre:
Free entry to this former
palace invites viewers to
explore a treasure trove of
Nordic culture. Denmark's
largest historical and
cultural museum has it all,
from Stone Age tools to
Victorian furniture. The
crown jewel? The 3,700-
year-old Sun Chariot.
natmus.dk

02 National Gallery of
Denmark, City Centre:
Founded on art collections
amassed by Danish
monarchs, the National
Gallery of Denmark brings
more than 700 years of
Western art and culture
together under one roof
– or rather two. Running
parallel are the museum
of 1896 and the modernist
extension of 1998, a stark
contrast of old and new.
smk.dk

03 NY Carlsberg Glyptotek,
City Centre: Brewing
magnate and art collector
Carl Jacobsen's museum
is an architectural feat: a
winter garden surmounted
by a glass dome sits at
the centre, sandwiched
between two buildings.
Inside it's all about ancient
Mediterranean cultures,
as well as Danish and
French art from the 19th
century. Don't miss the
rare Degas bronzes.
glyptoteket.dk

04 Museum of Copenhagen,
Vesterbro: The authority
on the city's history from
antiquity to present. The
museum moved from the
attic of city hall to the
former premises of the
Royal Shooting Society
in Vesterbro in the 1950s
and is now closed before
relocation to the city
centre in spring 2018.
cphmuseum.kk.dk

Off the wall

Den Frie's exhibits are weird and wonderful

⑥

Kunstforeningen GL Strand,
City Centre
Wide-angle lens

Across the canal from Slotsholmen, this art institution (which also has a cinema) hosts six to eight exhibitions a year. In recent years it has flown somewhat under the radar but the 2016 Mario Testino photography exhibition put it firmly back on the cultural map. The history of the gallery dates from 1825 when Kunstforeningen (The Art Society) was founded to introduce art to a wider public.

The courtyard is an oasis in the city centre; stop by for a glass of wine beneath its white sails.
48 Gammel Strand, 1202
+45 3336 0260
glstrand.dk

④

Den Frie Centre of Contemporary Art, City Centre
Rebel art

If you're after something offbeat, try this space that's home to Denmark's oldest artists' association: Den Frie Udstilling. Inspired by Paris's Salon des Refuses, it was founded in 1891 as an alternative to the juried spring exhibition at the Academy Charlottenborg. It is a platform for experimental artists whose creations wouldn't hang comfortably in public museums or commercial art galleries. The Greek and Egyptian-themed pavilion that the association is housed in is as quirky as the art.
1 Oslo Plads, 2100
+45 3312 2803
denfrie.dk

⑤

Cisternerne, Frederiksberg
Underground scene

In its day this reservoir held about 16 million litres of drinking water but by 1981 it was disused and drained. Fifteen years later the cave – complete with stalagmites and stalactites – began life as a gallery.

Exhibitions are site-specific (near 100 per cent humidity rules out paintings and drawings), with artists invited to create unique installations. "It has to be a symbiosis of art with the space," says director Astrid la Cour. "When it all comes together it is one of the most magical experiences. The rooms pose a challenge but add so much."
Søndermarken, 2000
+45 3073 8032
cisternerne.dk

⑦

Fotografisk Center, Vesterbro
Snap judgments

Fotografisk Center was founded in 1996 by Danish photographer Lars Schwander with the aim of promoting photography as both art and a documentary medium. Today it sits in a cavernous former warehouse in the old brown-brick section of the Meatpacking District.

The centre hosts six to eight shows a year and welcomes both international and homegrown talent. Danish artist Tina Enghoff's 2013 exhibition *Migrant Documents* is emblematic of the gallery's engagement with salient issues.
16 Staldgade, 1799
+45 3393 0996
photography.dk

Art day trips
Get out of town

2

Louisiana Museum of
Modern Art, Humlebaek
Natural resources

Open and uplifting, Louisiana is
an art museum founded in 1958
by Knud W Jensen, who had made
his fortune in the cheese industry.
What makes this museum unique
is the interplay between art, nature
and architecture, as seen in its
small-scale modernist buildings
that zigzag through the grounds.

In the Giacometti gallery, four
bronzes sit alongside Francis
Bacon's "Man and Child" in front
of a huge window that overlooks a
lake. The overall effect is described
by director Poul Erik Tøjner as
"almost a *Gesamtkunstwerk*: an
artistic totality". Calder and Arp
sculptures populate the extensive
gardens, exhibitions build on the
strong collection of pop art, and
the café is a destination in itself,
with sweeping views of the park-
like surroundings.
13 Gammel Strandvej, 3050
+45 4919 0719
louisiana.dk

1

Ordrupgaard Museum,
Charlottenlund
Blooming beauty

Once Wilhelm and Henny Hansen's
country home, this museum came
into being in 1953. The garden room
is devoted to Vilhelm Hammershøi,
a painter of poetic and almost
monochrome interiors, while a wing
designed by Zaha Hadid, made of
black lava concrete and glass, holds
temporary shows. A sculpture park is
dotted with works by Olafur Eliasson
and Jeppe Hein, and architect and
designer Finn Juhl's home (*see page
119*) is next door. Take a bike on
the train to Ordrup station and ride
from there.
110 Vilvordevej, 2920
+45 3964 1183
ordrupgaard.dk

(1)
Etage Projects, City Centre
Pushing boundaries

It's no surprise that Maria Foerlev (*pictured*) is at the centre of the city's art-and-design scene: the Danish dealer grew up in a house built by Arne Jacobsen, the father of modern design, so her good taste was somewhat predetermined. After studying fine and decorative arts at Sotheby's Institute of Art in London, then architecture at the Danish Royal Academy, she found herself torn between art, design and architecture so decided to focus on the grey area in between.

Foerlev opened Etage Projects – a gallery-cum-workshop that hosts exhibitions, lectures and events – in her hometown's art district in 2013. Via the works of interdisciplinary artists such as artist-and-designer duo Pettersen & Hein, the gallery breaks down the boundaries between traditional artistic practices.
15E Borgergade, 1300
+45 2623 3240
etageprojects.com

(2)
Galleri Nicolai Wallner, Vesterbro
Personal best

Nicolai Wallner founded his eponymous gallery in the city centre in 1993; he later moved it to the neighbourhood of Vesterbro and today – housed in a cavernous former lorry garage – it is one of the city's largest spaces dedicated to presenting the works of contemporary artists.

Wallner is anything but picky when it comes to mediums but his choice of who to represent is personal and often dates back to the gallery's conception: Scottish visual artist David Shrigley has been part of the line-up since 1997.
68 Ny Carlsberg Vej, 1760
+45 3257 0970
nicolaiwallner.com

(3)
Andersen's Contemporary,
City Centre
It takes two

One gallery was not enough for Andersen's Contemporary, which opened a second space in Copenhagen in 2016. The original spot among the auction houses on Bredgade presents smaller works, while the new one – a short stroll from the Danish Royal Palace in an apartment built between 1869 and 1870 – hosts larger exhibitions.

Andersen's Contemporary started in Berlin with a space called Andersen's Wohnung that was run from 1996 to 1999 by Danish artist Claus Andersen (*pictured*) and German artists Thilo Heinzmann and Anselm Reyle. After making his name in Germany, Andersen returned to Copenhagen in 2005. Today his galleries represent a range of international emerging and established artists who explore the role of art in contemporary society.
28 Bredgade, 1260
andersenscontemporary.dk

I've always been gifted at painting

⑤

V1 Gallery, Vesterbro
Street life

This relatively youthful gallery in the fashionable Meatpacking District was founded by designer Jesper Elg and photographer Peter Funch in 2002 to promote social and political discourse through art in all media. Keeping true to the formerly gritty character of its home neighbourhood, the gallery is known for a penchant for street art.

Celebrated Swedish artist André Saraiva is a regular exhibitor, and V1 was the first Scandinavian gallery to host graffiti artist Banksy in 2003.

69-71 Flaesketorvet, 1711
+45 3331 0321
v1gallery.com

④

Martin Asbaek Gallery, City Centre
In the mix

Art is in Martin Asbaek's blood: his parents run a gallery and one of his brothers is an art consultant (the other is actor Pilou). He opened this space in 2005 with a photography show – risky in Denmark back then – and his breakthrough came at Paris Photo. While photographers such as Trine Søndergaard are a mainstay, he's agnostic about the medium, even showing embroidery. "I love diversity but it has to be a complete experience," he says. For that reason he prefers solo shows in the main gallery, where the classical cornices offset contemporary art.

23 Bredgade, 1260
+45 3315 4045
martinasbaek.com

One for all
—
Martin Asbaek caters to lovers of all artistic media

Youth of today
—
With the aim of furthering the careers of emerging contemporary artists – both Danish and international – Galleri Christoffer Egelund always puts experimental and innovative works front and centre in its Bredgade space.
christofferegelund.dk

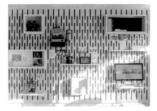

❶

Space10, Vesterbro
Reimagining the future

In 2013 design-focused creative
entrepreneur Carla Cammilla Hjort
and her team initiated a collaboration
with Ikea to set up a " future-living
lab" in which to test prototypes and
brainstorm concepts that would
create opportunities for a better and
more sustainable future. The result
was Space10.

Occupying a renovated ex-fishery
in the Meatpacking District, Space10
combines workdesks for a design
team, exhibition spaces and a
workshop kitted-out with tools.

The outfit offers a thought-
provoking programme of events
predicated on exploring "the future
of urban living"; they touch upon
everything from sustainable food
sources, health and wellbeing in
urban areas and explore the potential
of virtual-reality technologies. It also
hosts a residency programme for
visiting international designers and
forward-thinking individuals.
10 Flaesketorvet, 1711
space10.io

Hack of all trades
————

Among the many practical
workshops held at Space10
are those offering tips in how
to adapt – or "hack" – Ikea
furniture to suit individual
tastes and needs. Practising
what they teach, the team
have kitted out their office with
innovatively customised
items.

②
Huset-KBH, City Centre
Golden oldie

Founded in 1970, Huset-KBH is
Denmark's oldest and largest public
culture house. The popular venue in
Copenhagen's old town dates back
to the 18th century and was a cattle
shed in a previous life. Today the
multistorey building is the setting
for a hefty 1,500 annual events –
from live music and film screenings
to talks and theatre performances
– that take place across 10 thrown-
together stages.

Huset-KBH is a not-for-profit
cultural initiative that is run almost
entirely by volunteers. You'll
find entrances on both cobbled
Magstraede and Rådhusstraede, the
latter of which leads to a bustling
courtyard – the perfect place to enjoy
a beer. A boardgame café welcomes
visitors on the ground floor and a
tiny art-house cinema hosts a film
club upstairs. There's something for
everyone; pop in and explore.
13 Rådhusstraede, 1466
+45 2151 2151
huset-kbh.dk

Three more

01 Royal Danish Opera
House, Christianshavn:
The Royal Danish Opera
opened its Henning
Larsen-designed opera
house on Dock Island in
2005. Complete with
glass-and-steel façade,
the venue has six stages
and an underwater
rehearsal room.
kglteater.dk

02 Royal Danish Playhouse,
City Centre: Across
Nyhavn Canal is the
Royal Danish Playhouse,
inaugurated in 2008 as
a new stage for the
Royal Danish Theatre.
Designed by Copenhagen-
based architecture firm
Lundgaard & Tranberg, the
building has offices on its
upper level and a café and
restaurant in its foyer.
kglteater.dk

03 Black Diamond, City
Centre: Despite its
polished black-granite
exterior, the Black
Diamond is light and airy
within. The modern
extension of the historical
Royal Library features an
auditorium, concert hall,
two museums and a
bookshop. There's also
a restaurant and terrace
if your cultural drive
begins to wane.
kb.dk

Feeling blue?

Kind of Blue is a bar on
Ravnsborggade, but it is also a
venue for book-readings and/
or live music (all organised
by owner Claus Ploug). The
decor features vintage Eames
shell chairs and Jieldé lamps
against a backdrop of
blue walls.
kindofblue.dk

Cinemas
The big picture

①

Cinematek, City Centre
The reel thing

With the aim to protect, promote
and support Denmark's cinematic
tradition, the Danish Film Institute
is perhaps better seen as a museum
with a cinema attached. In its
building overlooking Rosenborg
Gardens, the institute's library,
videotheque, shop, film studio and
archive accompany three cinemas,
forming a world-class facility. More
than 60 Danish and international
films comprise the monthly
programme, with many shown
either in English or with subtitles.

Twice a month "Danish on
a Sunday" offers a classic movie
with a coffee and a Danish pastry;
or try the restaurant, named after
Henning Carlsen's 1966 *Hunger*.
55 Gothersgade, 1123
+45 3374 3400
dfi.dk

How about
a nice film
instead of
a roller
coaster?

Copenhagen on screen

01 Hans Christian Andersen, 1952: This musical fairytale follows the titular poet as he travels from a small town to Copenhagen's Royal Danish Theatre. Many of Andersen's stories appear, including *The Little Mermaid*.

02 Pusher, 1996: Nicolas Winding Refn's thriller spirals through the city's criminal underworld. The story of a drug deal gone wrong reveals a darker but no less sleek side to the Danish capital.

03 The Killing, 2007: Created by Søren Sveistrup and originally called *Forbrydelsen* (*The Crime*), *The Killing* paved the way for Scandinavian crime series to come. The story unfolds across the Danish capital, from Police HQ to city hall.

04 Borgen, 2010: This drama takes Danish coalition politics as its subject and Christiansborg Palace – nicknamed *Borgen* ("the Castle") and home to all three branches of the government – as its gloomy backdrop.

05 The Bridge, 2011 Hans Rosenfeldt's crime-ridden series sees a Swedish police detective working alongside a Danish inspector. The action begins between the two countries on the 16km Øresund Bridge.

06 The Danish Girl, 2015: Waterfront Nyhavn was transformed to look like 1920s Copenhagen in this biopic inspired by the lives of Danish painters Gerda Wegener and Lili Elbe (one of the first recorded recipients of gender reassignment surgery).

Grand Theatre, City Centre
Name of the game

This is a grand institution, from the gold signage over the door to its prime position near city hall. The red-brick building was completed by Danish architect Anton Rosen in 1910 and the first cinema on-site, Empire Theatre, opened in 1913.

Through its retro foyer, the cinema now has six digital screens that show the latest Danish releases, European films and independent productions. There's a focus on French classics, which Prince Henrik regularly attends. As it happens, he's a patron; a grand gesture indeed.
8 Mikkel Bryggers Gade, 1460
+45 3315 1611
grandteatret.dk

③
Vester Vov Vov, Vesterbro
Wine as you watch

Named after *Vester Vov-Vov* (*At the North Sea*), a Danish silent film from 1927, this charming local art cinema and café has been making waves in Copenhagen's film industry since opening in 1975. Originally a single screen run by a group of film students, Vester Vov Vov now features two digital cinema halls that show mostly European films, documentaries and US independent pictures.

The 1897 building started out as a Roman bathhouse before being converted into a tea room. Fortunately, tea and cake are still served at the café in the foyer – take time to admire the mosaic ceiling and the walls decorated with vintage film posters – and you can also enjoy a coffee (or glass of wine) as you watch a film.
5 Absalonsgade, 1658
+45 3324 4200
vestervovvov.dk

Live entertainment
Right here, right now

①
Bremen Teater, City Centre
Culture club

"Calling it a theatre is a misnomer," says managing director Jesper Majdall. "It's more like a culture house but that sounds so institutional." Whether you're watching comedy, concerts or theatre, Bremen Teater should feel like "your place for the evening".

Majdall and his partners took over the space in 2011 but retained some of its 1970s charm (there's a photo in the foyer of former owner Simon Spies in a leopard-print ensemble). A crowd aged 25-plus hits the Natbar disco on Fridays and Saturdays; expect to queue.
39-41 Nyropsgade, 1602
+45 3032 4090
brementeater.dk

②
The Standard, City Centre
Young and old

Jazz pianist Niels Lan Doky returned from Paris to partner with entrepreneur Claus Meyer and open The Standard in a former ferry terminal in 2013. The Jazz Club upstairs builds on Copenhagen's vibrant jazz scene in a chic space that evokes bars of old with recording-quality acoustics.

Having played with the greats during a career that has spanned 30 years, Lan Doky now wants to foster the next generation of jazz aficionados. His New Legacy concerts mix "extremely talented" young musicians with performances from old masters such as trumpeter Randy Brecker. Lan Doky says performing there is an intense experience for the young talent he features: "They're in the same room, playing the same repertoire for four to five weeks, so they develop further and quicker."
44 Havnegade, 1058
+45 7214 8808
thestandardjazzclub.com

Four more

01 Vega, Vesterbro: This music and party venue hosts about 250 concerts a year. Its two stages – one big and mainstream, the other more intimate – double as dance floors for nights of mostly electronic and house. *vega.dk*

02 Sigurdsgade & SGRD NTKLB, Nørrebro: This music venue and nightclub hosts every kind of night, from house to soul. Pop in on a Funky Friday from 21.00 until 04.00, or on a summer evening stop by its fairy-light-festooned rooftop bar. *sigurdsgade.com*

03 Pumpehuset, City Centre: This 1850s building has two stages for 600 and 400 guests respectively, with a focus on electronic and hip-hop. There's also a garden for concerts. *pumpehuset.dk*

04 Loppen, Christianshavn: Danish for "flea", Loppen is a small venue in Freetown Christiania that has featured emerging and established artists since 1973. Candles make for a casual vibe. *loppen.dk*

①

Newspapers and magazines
Read all about it

While English-language magazines are easy to find in the Danish capital, newspapers in anything but the national dialect are scarce. We've rounded up the best of both.

It's no surprise that design is the focus of one or two Copenhagen publications. **①** *Space Magazine* is about the "universal and sometimes extravagant" subject of living and is full of in-depth reports and cutting-edge photography. For more of a general lifestyle read opt for **②** *Oak: The Nordic Journal*; themed issues explore the Nordic way of life through culture, food and design.

Newspaper-wise, leading daily **③** *Politiken* has Danish-speakers covered. The broadsheet also has online English content but most English-speaking Copenhageners get their digital news at *thelocal.dk*.

The linguistically talented can also try **④** *Berlingske*, Denmark's oldest paper still in production.

Fashionistas should seek out **⑤** *Dansk*, an English-language magazine that covers both the international and Danish fashion scenes. And we finish as we began – with design. By popular demand there is now an English edition of Rum: **⑥** *Rum/International* is published monthly as a bookazine and includes interviews with designers and features on homes with interesting histories.

No, I can't read Danish but holding 'Politiken' makes me look clever

Radio

01 P3: This popular radio station specialises in rock and pop from artists both established and emerging – and has an audience of listeners largely under 30. A national station operated by the Danish Broadcasting Corporation (DR) – whose TV arm produced *The Killing* et al – it's broadcast on FM, DAB and internet radio. It also hosts entertainment shows, covers major sporting events and has hourly news bulletins.
dr.dk/p3

02 P6 Beat: Indie, alternative and rock lovers, look no further. Also operated by DR, P6 Beat focuses on underground music and is Denmark's leading alternative radio station.
dr.dk/p6beat

03 Radio24syv: Privately owned, publicly funded network Radio24syv launched in 2011. The new model for public radio takes its cue from US talk shows, with current affairs, cultural chat and tongue-in-cheek talk that's driven by panel discussions and phone-ins. Spontaneous and inclusive – with a healthy dose of wit and wisdom.
radio24syv.dk

Monocle 24
—
It would be remiss not to mention Monocle's own radio station, which features programmes ranging from daily news to our own design show 'Section D'. Listen online at *monocle.com/radio* or download the podcasts on iTunes or SoundCloud.

Design and architecture
—— Planning ahead

In less than 20 years, Copenhagen's skyline has changed dramatically. While you can still enjoy historic architecture and design, the city has become distinctly forward-looking. Much of the credit belongs to Jan Gehl, whose work on improving cities and their liveability has even birthed the term "Copenhagenisation". His philosophy that urban planning should focus on human needs epitomises the capital's shift in emphasis from cars to bicycles and pedestrianisation, and dovetails with the city's target of becoming carbon neutral by 2025. Projects such as Superkilen park build on the recommendation that no homes should be further than 300 metres from green space, while the VM Mountain project actually integrates the green into the houses. And with the city's waterside attributes now celebrated, there's been a surge in harbourside projects, from Olafur Eliasson's Cirkelbroen to the BLOX building by Rem Koolhaas.

City shapes
Striking structures

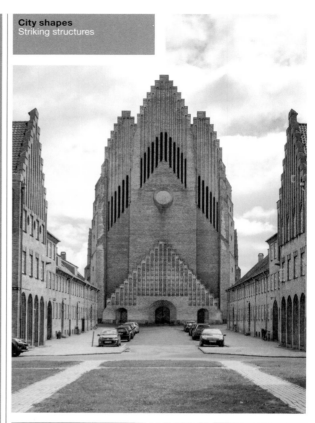

①

Grundtvig's Church, Bispebjerg
Awe-inspiring design

Constructed from some six million biscuit-coloured bricks, this monolithic church towers like a rocket ship over the quiet residential streets that surround it.

Designed by Peder Vilhelm Jensen-Klint in 1913 (although not finished until 1940, after his death) it's a rare example of religious expressionist architecture, and a pilgrimage for design enthusiasts.

Each element of the interior has been carefully considered, from the neat rows of beechwood-and-wicker chairs – designed for the church by the architect's son Kaare Klint (*see page 106*) – to the suspended light fittings, soaring columns and minimalist wooden hymn boards.

Note the seemingly incongruous four-masted model ship floating above the south aisle: votive ships are common in Danish churches but this is the largest example in the country.
14B På Bjerget, 2400
+45 3581 5442
grundtvigskirke.dk

②
Børsen, City Centre
Taking stock

The privately owned Danish stock exchange is closed to the public but with an exterior like this you're not short on things to look at. The copper roof and 56-metre-tall spire – formed from the entwined tails of four dragons – are well-known city landmarks. Stroll the length of the richly embellished red-brick building and you'll come face to face with equally eye-catching details: individuals peek out of pediments above windows and bare-chested figures top ornate columns.

Børsen reflects the tastes of its royal patron, Christian IV, who commissioned the grand building to reflect the importance of increased trade and commerce in Denmark. It was erected on the eastern corner of Slotholmen between 1620 and 1624 by brothers Lorenz and Hans van Steenwinckel, and assumed its current appearance in 1883.
1 Børsgade, 1217
+45 3374 6573
borsbygningen.dk

It doesn't need a bird's-eye-view to see that bridge is unusual

③
Police Headquarters, City Centre
Arresting sight

Hack Kampmann's 1924 behemoth is singular in its blend of classicism with modernist austerity, described by one critic as a "visual fist".

The shortest side has a portico of Vitruvian proportions, inspired by the Tabularium (the records office of ancient Rome) and leading to a circular courtyard encompassed by an ionic colonnade; examine its underside to find Greek meanders (decorative motifs) – touches of delicate finery amid the severity. Further inside is a smaller courtyard divided by a temple-like hall of Corinthian columns culminating in Einar Utzon-Frank's towering bronze statue the "Snake Killer".
Niels Brocks Gade, 1569

Niels Hansen Rasmussen
gymnasium, Frederiksberg
Fit for purpose

Niels Hansen Rasmussen, one of
the pioneers of Swedish gymnastics
in Denmark, built the Institute for
Voluntary Gymnastics for Men in
1898 as a place to improve mind
and body; to this day the inscription
over the door instructs visitors to
"straighten your back and speak the
truth". Architect PV Jensen-Klint, who
built the city's striking Grundtvig's
Church (*see page 102*), favoured
functionality and fine craftsmanship,
and the gym has stood the test of time:
it's still in use. Make an appointment
to use the facilities or sign up for an
exercise class.
51 Vodroffsvej, 1900
+45 3535 2019

Step back in time

Dragør, which lies 30 minutes'
drive south of the capital,
dates back to the 12th century,
later becoming a fishing port.
Still operating today, its unique
aesthetic is equally important:
the quaint cobbled streets,
thatched roofs and colourful
houses are treasures of Danish
rustic architecture.

Harbourside buildings
On the waterfront

Copenhagen Opera House, Holmen
Power player

For some Danes the Copenhagen
Opera House, with its cantilevered
roof the size of three football fields,
is a monument to the hubris of its
donor: Denmark's richest man,
Arnold Maersk Mc-Kinney Møller.
"God, King and Maersk," they
quip because the late shipping
magnate demanded his opera
house be built on the capital's most
prized site: on the axis through
Amalienborg Palace square to
the Marble Church.
    Mc-Kinney Møller hired revered
architect Henning Larsen and then
ran roughshod over him to such
an extent that Larsen apologised for
the "toaster", which opened in
2005. But the sheer pleasure of
experiencing a performance in the
main auditorium's warm maple shell
has won people over. The architect
died proud in 2013.
10 Ekvipagemestervej, 1438
+45 3369 6969
kglteater.dk

*I think shooting
these buildings
calls for a
boat*

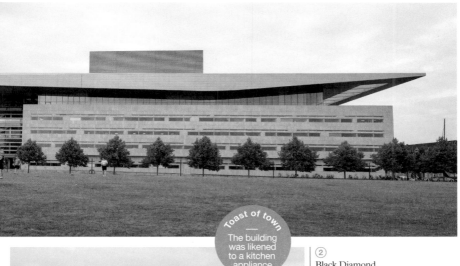

Toast of town
The building was likened to a kitchen appliance

②
Black Diamond
Harbourside sparkler

Its angular dark-marble façade has garnered this 1999 extension of the Royal Danish Library its apt moniker. Designed by Schmidt Hammer Lassen Architects, the chunky yet sleek structure is perched on the waterfront and houses not only reading rooms but dining areas, an auditorium and art galleries.

An expanse of glass in its front floods the 24-metre-high atrium with light. Inside, suspended bridges and wave-shaped balconies give the foyer an airy feel: at the back an 18-metre-wide walkway seamlessly connects to the old library building.
1 Søren Kierkegaards Plads, 1016
+45 3347 4747
kb.dk

New projects

The harbourside area is set to be changed further still with the development of a number of planned projects. Among the most striking is Rem Koolhaas's Blox, a building and urban space near to the Black Diamond (*see page 105*). The design is predicated on what Koolhaas calls Copenhagen's "harbour modernism" and a "hyper-clean, modern and polite" response to its existing neighbours. The visually low-key glass-and-steel edifice is underpinned by a socially aware commitment to foster interaction among its users. The Danish Architecture Centre opens in the complex in 2017.

Another upcoming project is Nordhavn, an ambitious century-defining plan to create a "sustainable city of the future" on the formerly industrial peninsula to the north of the city, for 40,000 residents and 40,000 workers. It's a 50-year project but you can already get a taste via its completed efforts: UN City, converted silos Portland Towers, and CIS Nordhavn with its façade of solar panels. Cycle pundits doubt, however, that the two towers constituting Steven Holl's LM Project will retain their elevated 17th-floor bicycle bridge linking the buildings.
blox.dk
nordhavnen.dk

Park and swim

Kvaesthus is a new urban space next to the Royal Danish Playhouse that combines a 15,000 sq m outdoor event space with an underwater carpark. It was designed by Copenhagen-based Lundgaard & Tranberg Arkitekter.
kvaesthusprojektet.dk

Modernism
Form follows function

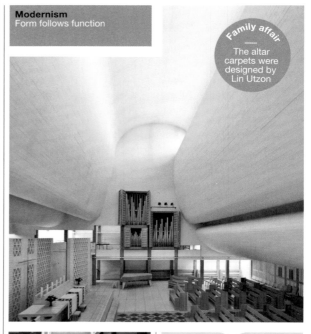

Family affair
—
The altar carpets were designed by Lin Utzon

①
Bagsvaerd Church, Bagsvaerd
Wedded bliss

Completed in 1976, this church was Jørn Utzon's first work after the Sydney Opera House. Its magnificence lies in its marriage of forms: the harsh orthogonal exterior of cast concrete, aluminium and ceramic gives way to a curved ceiling that rises like a rolling cloud above the altar. The ceiling contrasts with the straight lines of the beechwood pews, the rectangular choir stall and concrete pillars. More brilliant is Utzon's use of shapes to control light, entering primarily at the top of the ceiling and softly sinking along the curvature.
14-16 Taxvej, Bagsvaerd, 2880
+45 4498 4141
bagsvaerdkirke.dk

Kaare Klint

Kaare Klint's pronouncement that "form follows function" is a founding tenet of modernism. Initially a furniture designer, he created his first piece, the Faaborg Chair, at the age of 26, and was a key figure in founding the furniture school at the Royal Academy of Fine Arts in Copenhagen in 1923. He valued functionality, quality of materials, and understanding of form and purpose – principles seen in his 1933 Safari Chair, which is easily constructed and deconstructed without tools.

In the second half of the 20th century, while many frowned at modernism, Klint embraced it, finding a following in the likes of Børge Mogensen and Poul Kjaerholm who would bring about the Golden Age of Danish design and creation.

②
Lagkagehuset, Christianshavn
Concrete confection

Designed by Edvard Thomsen,
a devotee of Denmark's Funkis
movement, this 1930s block made
waves for its lack of adornment.
Critics dubbed it Lagkagehuset or
"layered cake house" for its yellow-
and-white stripes; while adhering
to modernism's functional lines, it's
a confection of bricks and plaster
painted to look like concrete.

Note the wraparound balconies
and corner details on the Apothek
and Lagkagehuset bakery, named
after its first home. To experience its
light-filled space go to the first-floor
library, which has been there since
day one.
45-47 Torvegade, 1400
ablagkagehuset.dk

③
Dronningegården, City Centre
Form and function

This residential complex of four
L-shaped buildings surrounding
a peaceful garden has pleasing
symmetry. The red-brick structure
was designed by Danish functionalist
master Kay Fisker and completed
in 1958 after a 15-year gestation.
Slanted-roof units make the most of
façade space with a compact grid of
balconies while the interconnecting
blocks feature a rationalist pattern
of alternating square windows and
slightly receded balconies.

Other than lining the balconies'
profiles, yellow bricks are used in
subtle cross-shaped decorations that
make for the only decoration on the
strictly geometric structure.
Dronningegården, 1304

Arne Jacobsen
The design all-rounder

1

Danmarks Nationalbank, City Centre
Money matters

Denmark's central bank moved its
HQ from Slotsholmen to Holmen's
Canal in 1870, and in 1961 several
leading architects were invited to
submit proposals for its expansion.
Arne Jacobsen won, and the building
as we know it was built between 1965
and 1978, with Copenhagen-based
architecture and design practice
Dissing + Weitling completing the
project after Jacobsen's death in 1971.

The clean-cut Danmarks
Nationalbank appears to be
impenetrable, behind a curtain-like
façade. On Havnegade, however,
is a modest entrance that leads into
the lobby, open to the public on
weekdays from 09.00 to 16.00. The
20-metre-high wedge-shaped space
is lined – like the façade – with light
Porsgrunn marble. A sculptural
steel-and-glass staircase – dotted
with coin-like lights – ascends to
the building's six floors.
5 Havnegade, 1093
+45 3363 6363
nationalbanken.dk

Modernist master
————

Functionalism pioneer Arne
Jacobsen was born in 1902 and
studied architecture under Kay
Fisker and was later influenced
by Bauhaus director Walter
Gropius. He became one of the
world's most successful furniture
designers; to date his Series 7
chair has sold more than five
million units.

③
Skovshoved Petrol Station,
Charlottenlund
Fuel for thought

Arne Jacobsen's 1938 seaside
petrol station, 10km north of the
capital, was commissioned by oil
company Texaco but never went
beyond the prototype. It features
white Messien tiles topped by
a concrete canopy to protect
customers from the sun – a true
token of Jacobsen's functionalism.
24 Kystvejen, Charlottenlund, 2920

②
Bellavista Estate and Bellevue
Theatre, Klampenborg
Beach belles

The popular beach resort 10km
north of the capital is home to
Arne Jacobsen's 1934 Bellavista
estate. The commission was
one of the first after his trip to
Germany, where he was inspired
by Walter Gropius's Bauhaus
school. Its trademarks are apparent
in Bellavista: a U-shaped layout
with large windows and integrated
curved balconies affords sunlight
and a sea view for each apartment;
meanwhile the split-level design
allows for two living rooms in each
flat. On the beach below are
Jacobsen's delightfully light-hearted
lifeguard towers.

His Bellevue Theatre is
next door, built two years later
but matching the estate in
its whitewashed appearance.
Originally conceived as a summer
venue, the flat roof is designed
to slide open on warm evenings.
The inside is equally spectacular:
yellow-and-blue striped walls
echo the summer season, and a
curved, wooden rear enhances
the acoustics. Today it hosts year-
round performances.
*419-443 Strandvejen and
451 Strandvejen, Klampenborg, 2930
+45 7020 2096
bellevueteatret.dk*

④
Radisson Blu Royal Hotel,
Vesterbro
Passion project

Arne Jacobsen's 1960 hotel project
is the epitome of his belief in "total
design": he created everything from
the lighting and chairs to the cutlery
and curtains. Though the hotel has
been updated, Room 606 is in its
original condition. The 22-storey
building was also the first – and
last – skyscraper in the city centre.
radissonblu.com

*Arne Jacobsen
got his idea for the
Swan chair from me!*

❶
Centre for Cancer
and Health, Nørrebro
Healthy environment

Design firm Nord Arkitekter tailored
this 2011-built facility for cancer
patients towards well-being and
a homely atmosphere. Instead of
convoluted signs, sterile waiting
rooms and reception halls, you'll
find tall ceilings, parquetted floors
and large windows that create a
comfortable environment. Several
houses grant privacy; each one is
asymmetrical, affording a sense of
individuality. The houses converge
on a central courtyard where patients
can enjoy each other's company or
tend to the popular vegetable garden.
45 Nørre Allé, 2200
+45 8220 5800
kraeftcenter-kbh.dk

② Axel Towers, Vesterbro
Virtuous circles

Proving you *can* put a round building into a square hole, Axel Towers is testament to progressive council planners. Defeated by trying to design a building that fit neatly on the square site opposite Tivoli Gardens, Lundgaard & Tranberg suggested a building detached from its neighbours. Five fused circular towers of differing heights deliver office space, but also a landmark in an urban garden instead of a squat box. "We put a sculpture in the middle of a square that you can move around," says project leader Michael Kvist of the towers clad in zinc-coated copper that will patinate to a deep bronze.
2-4 Axeltorv, 1609

Residential
Homegrown housing

① Potato Rows, Østerbro
All together now

When this enclave of townhouses was built in the 19th century the focus was on community, not aesthetic. The passing of time has improved both, even though it is a very different community to that for which it was intended. Dubbed Kartoffelraekkerne or "potato rows", the 480 terraced homes were built by the Workers Construction Society in the 1870s and are now the much sought-after preserve of the well-heeled. There are street picnics, children's teepees, tricycles and other effects strewn about that act as traffic calmers and claim the area for pedestrians.
Wiedeweltsgade, 2100

④
Brumleby, Østerbro
Light relief

Brumleby was conceived in the wake of the 1853 cholera epidemic in order to provide new, more sanitary dwellings. The estate was designed by architect Michael Gottlieb Bindesbøll and completed in 1872. The humble two-storey neoclassical-style homes are now some of the most sought-after real estate in the city.

57 Osterbrogade, 2100

③
VM houses, Ørestad
Pointed design

Seen from above, these two 2005 apartment blocks appear as the letters V and M, tessellating without touching. Designed by Bjarke Ingels Group, JDS and Plot, who would later collaborate on the VM Mountain (*see page 113*), they use limited space and a small construction spend to provide maximum light and views.

The most eye-catching elements from ground level are the jagged balconies, another technique that promotes natural light to the interior. Inside, to further maximise light and airiness, all the apartments consist of just one room; there are no partitions to break up the spaces.

55 Orestads Boulevard, 2300
vmhusene.dk

②
Torpedohallen, Christianshavn
Design bombshell

This skeletal-looking structure in the former military area of Holmen (opposite Christiania, itself an ex-army base) was once a torpedo-boat shipyard, built in 1952. Its purpose today is far from martial: the building was converted into 67 luxury apartments by Tegnestuen Vandkunsten Archtiects in 2003.

All that remains from the original design are the concrete beams and columns that designate the building profile. The ample space and large windows make for comfortable living and residents can park their own private boats along the internal water basin where torpedoes would have once been lowered.

1-11 Galionsvej, 1437

Elevated ideals
———
A residents' lift moves up the slope at an angle

⑤
VM Mountain, Ørestad
Peak achievement

Set between the ample Ørestads Boulevard and a quiet canal, the VM Mountain block has two very distinct faces. Street-side, a huge multi-level carpark for apartment residents is hidden away behind a shiny metal façade, punctured with holes that form a pattern recalling Mt Everest. But at the rear of the carpark the 80 residential flats cascade down towards the canal with terraces and roof gardens that face into the sun. A collaboration between Bjarke Ingels Group, JDS and Plot, the end result won best housing at the 2008 World Architecture Festival.
55 Ørestads Boulevard, 2300
jdsa.eu

(6)
Tietgenkollegiet, Ørestad
Study in community

The Tietgen Residence Hall works to encourage community while still providing for individuals. Housing almost 400 students, the circular building, designed by Lundgaard & Tranberg, stands seven storeys tall with a planted courtyard in its centre. Five vertical sections sliced from the main ring allow sight lines and access to the courtyard, over which the common areas – the kitchens and meeting spaces – cantilever and are freely visible. Students in one part of the ring can see into the others and walk easily from section to section. No corridor has a dead end, inviting interaction between different parts of the block.
10-18 Rued Langgaards Vej, 2300

Outdoor and infrastructure
Open-air attractions

Cirkelbroen, Christianshavn
Round trip

"Cirkelbroen celebrates pedestrians," says architect Olafur Eliasson, who designed this bridge based on childhood memories of fishing boats moored so closely together, people could cross the harbour by walking from one to another. Completed in 2015, Cirkelbroen comprises of five circular platforms, staggered in a zigzag pattern, and each with its own "mast". It crosses the Christianshavns Kanal, and can be interpreted from the side as either a series of boats alongside each other, or one five-masted vessel. Two of the five circles are capable of swinging outwards, to allow taller vessels to pass through.
Christianshavns Kanal, 1411

Christiania ideals
—
Planning regulations don't apply to the hippie commune of Freetown Christiania – they are impossible to enforce. The result is a mishmash of makeshift homes made from recycled materials. It's worth a wander to take a peek at the DIY ingenuity.

② Kalvebod Bølge, Vesterbro

Where beach meets boardwalk

Situated in what was an unloved part of the inner harbour, Kalvebod Bølge (Kalvebod Waves) is the urban counterpart to the manmade "beach" across the water at Islands Brygge. Conceived by JDS Architects and Klar, the undulating boardwalk juts out into the harbour to catch the sun where the shadows from nearby office towers don't reach. Kayakers have their own slide while the promenade's curves are popular with skaters – who sometimes end up in the drink.

Kalvebod Brygge, 1560

Activity centre
—
Red Square extends from Nørrebro sports hall

④
Cykelslangen, Vesterbro
Viper trail

For years, cycling from the harbour bridge to the highway meant avoiding pedestrians and stairs. The Bicycle Snake, which opened in 2014, offers a cycle-only alternative. Designed by Dissing + Weitling, the 190-metre-long track is suspended over the harbour, its surface a tasteful hazard-jacket orange. Oh, and it's shaped like a snake.
København V, 1560

③
Superkilen, Nørrebro
Park life

Nørrebro is home to about 60 nationalities, and this 30,000 sq m park, the result of a collaboration between Bjarke Ingels Group, landscape architect firm Topotek1 and artists' group Superflex, was devised to celebrate that diversity. It's made up of three areas: Red Square is for fitness activities; the Black Market is where locals meet; and Green Park appeals to families.

On any given day you'll see skaters scooting around free children's sport classes, grey-haired men squabbling over chess on the purpose-built tables and buffed bodies on the outdoor gyms. It's a testament to thoughtful design.
208 Nørrebrogade, 2200

Design for life

Israels Plads is another of the city's strikingly well-considered civic areas. The large public square, overhauled by Sweco Architects in 2008, has sports courts and is used as an overspill area for drinkers and diners at the nearby Torvehallerne market.

By the sea
Ocean views

①
Kastrup Søbad Seawater
Lido, Kastrup
Swim in a sculpture

Sweden's White Arkitekter conceived
Kastrup Søbad as a "sculptural
dynamic form that can be seen
from the beach, the sea or the air".
A crescent-shaped wall of wooden
slats rises from 1.5 metres to 8
metres with a changing silhouette
as it encircles the baths. Everything
is unified by the African hardwood
azobé used for the wall, decks,
benches and jetty said to be as
resistant to saltwater as steel. Go on
a sunny day when kids jump or dive
from pontoons, decks or two boards.
301 Amager Strandvej, 2770
+45 3076 0235
taarnby.dk/oplev-taarnby/
idraetslivet-i-taarnby/kastrup-soebad

Den Blå Planet, Kastrup
Deep blue

Denmark's national aquarium is an
expression and physical embodiment
of its function: a whirlpool sucking
visitors below the sea. Created by
design firm 3XN, it won the Riba
European Award in 2014.

Five arms, incorporating tanks
and display areas, radiate out from a
central "eye". The exterior is clad in
more than 40,000 diamond-shaped
aluminium shingles that reflect
sea and sky. An innovative surface
finish both protects from the harsh
elements and allows rainwater runoff
to be collected and used in the
aquarium without further treatment.
1 Jacob Fortlingsvej, 2770
+45 4422 2244
denblaaplanet.dk

Design museums
Display homes

Museum pieces — Denmark's design gems are often on display

1

Designmuseum Danmark,
City Centre
That's a wrap

Housed in a converted 18th-century hospital, Designmuseum Danmark is anything but sterile. The rococo building wraps around a central garden, inviting viewers to walk from room to room along a timeline of talented Danish designers. Permanent exhibitions include the self-explanatory "Learning from Japan" and "Danish Design Now".

As well as admiring iconic pieces by the Danish design scene's leading lights, make sure you take a turn around the fully stocked museum shop. If you want to dig deeper, the piled-high library is open to everyone. Alternatively, if you want a breather, Klint Café does a delicious open-faced sandwich – and on Wednesdays when the museum stays open until 21.00, it offers a reasonably priced (and rather tasty) three-course meal.
68 Bredgade, 1260
+45 3318 5656
designmuseum.dk

②

Danish Architecture Centre,
City Centre
Building interest

As well as regular exhibitions and the Copenhagen X Gallery, which covers dozens of sites of architectural significance, the Danish Architecture Centre offers free guided tours in English (on Sundays, once you've paid the centre entrance fee). But the centre really comes into its own with its technology. The online Danish Architecture Guide allows you to select sites that take your fancy and compiles them into a tour. There is also a series of podwalks and podruns to introduce you to the city's architectural gems while you exercise.
27B Strandgade, 1401

Hmmm, I spy a Danish Modern masterpiece

③

Finn Juhl's Hus, Charlottenlund
A life's work

The house Finn Juhl built for himself in 1942 was a lab for his approach to interior design. He created furniture with an organic character – none went into production unless it worked in his home, which he designed from the "inside out", the function of the rooms determining the external façade.

A private donation put home and contents under Ordrupgaard Museum's stewardship in 2008. Take your time walking through, noting how Juhl grouped the furniture and used windows to frame views.
Ordrupgaard Museum
110 Vilvordevej, 2920
+45 3964 1183
ordrupgaard.dk

Iconic Danish designers

01 Nanna Ditzel: With husband Jørgen, Ditzel designed the rattan hanging egg chair – and was an important voice in Denmark's emerging postmodernist movement.

02 Poul Kjaerholm: The designer behind some of Republic of Fritz Hansen's most popular pieces had a fascination for steel: most of his iconic designs boast industrial-looking, thin metallic structures.

03 Verner Panton: His eponymous chair was a 1960s triumph and the embodiment of the Gamtofte-born designer's distinctive preoccupations: bright colours and an experimental approach to material and shapes.

04 Jacob Jensen: The Vesterbro native found fame with his industrial product design, especially for electronics company Bang & Olufsen.

05 Poul Henningsen: A theorethical approach to light design paid off in Henningen's renowned line for Louis Poulsen that bears his initials, notably his flower-like pendant.

06 Børge Mogensen: Aalborg-born Mogensen came to fame with simple designs aimed at the public. The chunky Spanish Chair remains his most accomplished piece.

07 Hans J Wegner: The Wishbone chair is perhaps the most famous of Wegner's designs but was only one of about 500 chairs he created.

08 Mogens Koch: The architect was fascinated by modularity and flexibility, principles applied, respectively, to his square bookshelf and folding chair.

 ①

Bronze and copper decorations
Copperhagen

Gaze across Copenhagen's skyline and you'll see countless patches of copper and bronze employed to decorate everything from church spires and grand domes to light filaments, street signs and bridge control towers. Exposure to salty breezes has resulted in pleasing patinas – depending on their age, structures may be green, red, brown or black. In a bid to seamlessly integrate new builds into the cityscape, many contemporary architects have pressed these old materials into service. There are even whole buildings clad in copper, such as Vesterbro's Axel Towers (*see page 111*) and the Nordea office building opposite Central Station.

③
Nyhavn, City Centre
Harbouring delights

The waterfront area of Nyhavn dates back to 1670 when a plan to connect the market of Kongens Nytorv with the sea sprouted taverns and brothels that served a heavy footfall of sailors and merchants. While most of the buildings on the south side of the canal date from 1770s, number 9 on the north side is the oldest in the area. Built in 1681, it stands unchanged, bar a requisite lick of bright blue paint.

Once a busy port, the harbour's commercial activity continued until it was all but abandoned after the Second World War. The mid 1960s saw a regeneration programme that got the party going again and, ironically, the large ships that once brought about Nyhavn's demise now secure the area's prosperity: that only small vessels can access the harbour makes for an untainted backdrop to a long summer evening.
1-71 Nyhavn, 1051
+45 3312 3233
nyhavn.com

④
Christiania Bike
Peddling pedalling

Designed in 1984 by Lars Engstrom, these tricycles have chassis that come equipped with front-mounted cargo boxes used to transport just about anything that needs moving, from children to groceries.

Expertly crafted and beautiful in their utilitarian simplicity, the bikes were awarded the Danish Design Centre's Classic Design Prize in 2010 for "well-deserved icon status". Elevating a bike to this level may seem strange to outsiders but it's indicative of the reverence Danes hold for their emblematic mode of transportation.
christianiabikes.com

②
Spires
Reach for the sky

Copenhagen's epithet, "the City of Spires", is well deserved. One of the most eye-catching is the copper decoration atop the Nikolaj Church (*pictured, top*), a 1909 reproduction of the original that dated back to the Renaissance. You also won't be able to miss the 60-metre dragon spire of Borsen (*see page 103*). It bears three golden crowns representing the countries of the former Scandinavian empire (Denmark, Norway, and Sweden) and is said to protect from fire. Or why not ascend the baroque spire of the Church of Our Saviour in Christianshavn (*pictured, above*)? It dates to 1752 and features a staircase winding up to its golden pinnacle.

That's the last time I get 'inspired' to fly to the top...

⑤
Hanging lamps
Bright idea

Created by municipal architects in 1977, these dome-shaped lights helped to define the capital, rendering the street lamppost-free. In 2015 more than 20,000 bulbs were replaced by green models to reduce energy consumption by 57 per cent. While their replacements are yet to be considered city icons, the new street lights respect classic Nordic design.

Sport and fitness
—— Get moving

As a whole, Denmark takes fitness seriously – its obesity rate is about half that of both Australia and the UK – and Copenhagen is no different.

More than anything it's the lifestyle that accounts for the city's trim, taut and terrific image; along with healthy eating, people get plenty of exercise simply by moving from place to place. While many choose to travel on foot, it's cycling that sets Copenhagen apart. There are bikes everywhere, with hundreds of kilometres of dedicated cycling lanes, making it an easy and affordable way to take in the city's sights while getting plenty of fresh air and a decent workout.

If two wheels are too many for you, there's no shortage of gyms and spas to get your heart rate up; we'll point you to the best options. There's also paddling and swimming, although doing laps is more the exception than the rule here; most just enjoy splashing around. And, of course, if you want to pamper yourself after working up a sweat, we've got you covered there too.

Watersports
Make a splash

(1)
Paddling, City Centre
Water view

The vast expanse of waterways in the centre of Copenhagen have seen an increase in kayaking in recent years. Offering a unique perspective on the city's best-loved sights, kayak tours typically last two hours and are usually at a relaxed pace. While there are a few operators to choose from, Kayak Republic has been in business for 10 years and offers short courses as well as guided tours. Its Nordic Food tour lasts three hours; a light paddle to sample fresh seafood around the harbour is followed by a mussels supper on its "floating beach" at Kayak Bar.
12 Børskaj, 1221
+45 2288 4989
kayakrepublic.dk

Lap it up
Fisketorvet is where serious swimmers head

②

Harbour baths, citywide
Get in lane

Swimming in the harbour was unthinkable 15 years ago when the water was so contaminated it was a health risk. Today it's pristine (if cold), with three harbour baths. Bear in mind that Copenhageners like jumping in the harbour more than swimming in it, so the baths are designed with fun in mind.

You can do laps in the pool at Islands Brygge but they're not orderly. Serious swimmers go to Fisketorvet's dedicated 50-metre pool. At Sluseholmen there are two pools for exercise and diving in a lagoon-like space. The baths are open from 1 June to 30 September.
Islands Brygge
14 Islands Brygge, 2300
+45 3089 0469
Fisketorvet
55 Kalvebod Brygge, 1560
+45 3089 0470
Sluseholmen
69 Ben Websters Vej, 2450
+45 5182 6379
teambade.kk.dk

Is it time for a doggy-paddle joke?

③

Amager Strandpark, Amager
Recreation all-rounder

At Amager, just 5km from the city centre, you can kayak, windsurf, kite-surf, play beach volleyball, shoot hoops, swim, snorkel and sunbathe. In summer the patrolled beaches are off limits to wind and kite-surfers. The Helgoland sea baths, rebuilt in 2008, are good for a peaceful swim.
Amager Strandvej, 2300
kk.dk/amagerstrandpark

①
Butcher's Lab Gym, Vesterbro
Beefing up

Butcher's Lab is certainly not
your conventional exercise setting.
The gym opened in 2008 and
moved into a former slaughterhouse
after a short stint set up in a luxury
apartment. The focus rotates
around the Workout of the Day:
an hour-long team session, held
up to eight times a day, involving
bodyweight and barbell exercises
(if you want to attend a drop-in
session it will cost you about €13).
If you prefer a solo workout it's best
to come by during the open-gym
hours scattered through the day.
22 Staldgade, 1699
+45 5370 9931
butchers.dk

Two more

01 Fitness DK, citywide:
This well-established gym
chain offers one and
three-day passes at
very reasonable rates.
There are squash courts
at the branch on the fourth
floor of the Radisson Blu
Scandinavia, while
wellness centres,
saunas and cafés are
commonplace in the other
locations across the city.
fitnessdk.dk

02 Fitness World, citywide:
Fitness World has a variety
of membership levels that
vary from night-time
access to just one studio,
to full access across all
fitness centres. Strength
training and bike fitness
courses are available.
fitnessworld.com

Cycling
Do the ride thing

Copenhagen has been working to
reduce the amount of car traffic for
years. Since 2009, about DKK2.8bn
(€377m) has been invested
nationwide into radical pro-cycling
initiatives, including the long-
distance networks of *cykelsuperstier*
paths that connect out-of-town
commuters to the city.
   Visitors are also well catered
for with the Bycyklen hire scheme.
Although its implementation wasn't
without hiccups (read high price
tags, delayed delivery and waning
demand), the electric bikes fitted
with GPS-enabled tablets are easy to
hire and can be found at about 105
stations citywide. Locals will spot
the chunky white bikes a mile off, so
blend in by respecting the following
points on etiquette and safety.

RULES OF THE ROAD
01 Never ride down a bike lane
in the wrong direction.
02 Always signal when you're
stopping by raising your right
hand to shoulder height, palm
facing forward.
03 Signal when turning and if
you're performing a left turn
across an intersection, follow
the pedestrians and complete a
box turn, all the while keeping
to the right of the lane.

DGI Byen, Vesterbro
Mixing business and pleasure

This centrally located business
and leisure centre comes complete
with a comprehensive swim centre
and well-stocked gym. The fitness
facilities are open to corporate
customers and the general public,
as well as guests of the adjacent
hotel. A day pass, including classes,
costs DKK65 (€9).

The 125 sq m gym – which
is kitted out for both strength
training and cardio – has 17 Cybex
machines, including seven that
focus on cardio workouts, and
offers a range of popular classes.

Sweat it out as you overlook the
pools below and then pop down
(via the shower) for a well-earned
dip. If regular workouts aren't your
speed, there's aqua-spinning and
water aerobics or – if you dare –
head to the diving pool, which is
accompanied by a climbing wall,
tower and trampoline.
65 Tietgensgade, 1704
+45 3329 8000
dgi-byen.com

Horses for courses

At the 107-year-old Mattssons
riding club in Klampenborg you
can hire a horse and explore
Arne Jacobsen's 1934 take on
a riding academy. Two-hour
group rides for skilled riders
head through the huge deer
park Jaegersborg Dyrehave.
mattssons-rideklub.dk

*Are you sure we all
benefit aerobically
from this?*

Grooming
A cut above

①
Barberen i Vognmagergade,
City Centre
Gentlemen only

When he became only the
third owner of this decades-old
barbershop, Jonas Shiran Larsen
knew he had to respect its heritage.

"It can't be trendy," says Larsen,
who took over in 2007. "I want it
to be as gentlemanly as possible
with a strong masculine feeling."
From its black glass and mirrors to
its three chairs, everything dates
back to 1937, when Egmont
Publishing installed a barber in
its new headquarters to ensure
executives could get a handy
haircut. Out the back there's
even a lift that heads up to the
executive offices. To maintain
decorum Larsen kits out his
barbers in bow ties and white
shirts, unusual attire for casual
Copenhagen. They cut hair, trim
beards and do clean shaves using
their 1937 product range.
19 Vognmagergade, 1120
+45 3312 6343
barb.dk

Four more

01 Amazing Space, city
centre: This spa, set in the
18th-century Hotel
D'Angleterre, was totally
redesigned in 2013 by
Space Copenhagen – the
team behind Noma. It now
features a distinctly Scandi
aesthetic. At your disposal
is a fitness suite that's fully
Technogym-equipped, and
an indoor swimming pool.
Those not staying in the
hotel are welcome but
must buy one of the many
treatments on offer.
amazing-space.dk

02 Carl's Barber
Shop, Østerbro
Old-school barbers are
a rare find but this one,
just north of the centre,
has been running for 75
years. A classic cut costs
around €65; you can book
in advance or drop in and
sample some craft beer
while you wait.
carlsbarbershop.dk

03 Gun-Britt Coiffure, City
Centre: Gun-Britt Zeller
opened her salon in 2010
and has been in the
hairdressing industry for
more than 50 years. The
house style is inspired by
renowned master Vidal
Sason; keen to impart
wisdom herself, Zeller
hosts masterclass courses
for aspirants in her
polished salon. No time for
a cut? Just check out the
in-house hair products.
gun-britt.dk

04 Dollface, City Centre:
Founded in 2007 by young
cosmetologist Lillie
Østergaard Steffensen,
this beauty salon caters to
both men and women,
offering everything from
classic haircuts and facials
to massages and full
osteopathy treatments.
dollface.dk

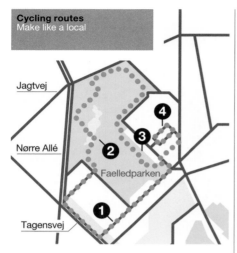

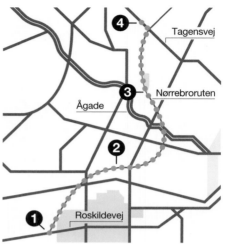

①

Faelledparken cycle
Parkland with a touch of history

This easy ride circles around Faelledparken, one of the
city's most popular recreational spaces, and includes a
nosy around the historic Brumleby estate (*see page 112*).

STARTING POINT: Blegdamsvej in Østerbro
DISTANCE: 5.75km

If you need some wheels, collect a bike from the
❶ *Bycyklen station* in front of the hospital on
Blegdamsvej. Then head south (150 metres) to Tagensvej
and turn right (it's best to cycle through the park). At
the end of the path, turn right and head for the road
leading between the buildings. You'll pass through some
gates into the park; turn left and follow the winding path
through the trees.
　　When you reach the lake, look to your right and
you'll see ❷ *Café Pavillonen*, a good spot for a hit of
caffeine. Continue on until you reach a bridge; cross
it and turn right. Soon the path will join a larger road;
turn right and at the major intersection cross and
continue straight ahead. Take the first left to continue
around the edge of the park, always keeping to the right.
At ❸ *Sansehaven* (a sensory garden) turn left and make
your way to main road Øster Allé.
　　Dismount and carefully cross the street. Turn
left and then immediately right onto multi-hued
Olufsvej, one of the city's quaintest streets. Turn left
at the end and you'll see the entrance to ❹ *Brumleby*.
Dismount and walk around the yellow-and-white former
housing that dates back to the 19th century.
　　Head back to Øster Allé and turn left. Turn right
at Blegdamsvej to return your bike. Another option is
to continue south to loop around the scenic lakes.

②

The green path cycle
Clever urban infrastructure

This Frederiksberg cycle path is primarily a means
for Copenhageners to get from A to B, but intelligent
planning makes it a pleasant and pretty ride through
the west.

STARTING POINT: Roskildevej in Frederiksberg
DISTANCE: 5.8km

Pick up a bike from the ❶ *Roskildevej/Borgmester
Fischersvej Bycyklen station* and cross the intersection
north to enter the cycle path. Once you pass the initial
housing block, the right-hand side will peter out to
a wall of shrubbery marking the boundaries of the
Solbjerg Kirkegård, which was founded in 1865 and
colloquially coined Pheasant Cemetery.
　　Follow the path north. After 1 km the path will
finish; cross Peter Bangs Vej and you'll see where
it picks up off Lindevangs Alle. Another diagonal
crossing, this time over Nordre Fasanvej, will follow.
The next stretch will take you past the manicured
❷ *Copenhagen Business School campus* to meet up with
Frederiksberg's decommissioned freight railway tracks.
　　Continue north along the bikeway and cross
the Åboulevarden pedestrian and bicycle bridge that
opened in 2008 as part of the city's Green Cycle
Route initiative. The final few kilometres are along
the meticulously manicured Nørrebroruten that leads
past ❸ *Nørrebroparken*. If the weather is good, food
trucks will be set up on the south corner of the park.
Cycle through the faded yet still striking playgrounds
of Superkilen (*see page 116*), pass the supersized Santa
Monica-inspired outdoor gym and break away from
the path at Tagensvej to head north and dock your
bike at ❹ *Bispebjerg Station*.

Running routes
Jog on

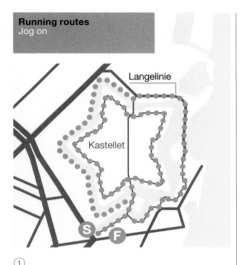

Langelinie

Kastellet

S F

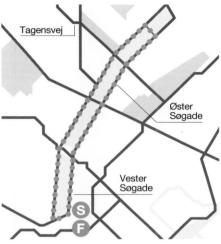

Tagensvej

Øster
Søgade

Vester
Søgade

S F

① Kastellet run
Star-studded route

DISTANCE: 4km
GRADIENT: Flat, with some sharp inclines
DIFFICULTY: Easy
HIGHLIGHT: Views from the ramparts, Danish royals
BEST TIME: Early morning
NEAREST METRO: Kongens Nytorv
NOTE: The inner loop is accessible from 06.00 to 22.00.

This involves two loops round the Kastellet fortress (built by Frederik III in 1662 to ward off the Swedes). Begin at the intersection of Grønningen and Esplanaden. Take the central path so the water is on your left. When you reach the bridge, don't cross; take the path to the right around St Alban's Church. Keep left, run past the fountain featuring the Norse goddess Gefjun and cross the bridge for views over the harbour to the right.

Continue down the path towards the boat masts in the distance. You're approaching Den Lille Havfrue (the Little Mermaid), Hans Christian Andersen's character, sculpted by Edvard Eriksen. Give it a glance, then bear left past the marina. The gradient will increase slightly. Keep left along the main road and continue as it begins to dip then curve sharply left; follow the horseshoe around and turn left at the intersection.

At the bridge, don't cross: take the gravel path to the right until you reach the bridge to the inner island, home to the Danish navy. Cross and pass through the tunnel. Take the steep track to your immediate left and head to the top of the ramparts, then turn right and jog around, enjoying the views. When you've completed an entire loop head back down the track at the side of the bridge and through the tunnel. Cross the bridge and continue straight to arrive back at the starting point.

② Lakes run
Water course

DISTANCE: 5.5km
GRADIENT: Flat
DIFFICULTY: Moderate
HIGHLIGHT: Glimpses of the Potato Row houses and other venerable residences
BEST TIME: Any time on a weekday
NEAREST METRO: Vesterport

This run starts outside the cylindrical Tycho Brahe Planetarium on the corner of Gammel Kongevej and Vester Søgade. Sticking to the right side of the footpath, head north along Sankt Jørgens Sø, the first in a series of three lakes to the west of the city centre. The lakes were built in the early 1500s to provide water to Copenhagen's expanding population. Depending on the season, along the eastern bank you'll pass under a verdant canopy of chestnut trees. At each major intersection you will have to veer away from the water slightly to cross at the lights. At the end of Peblinge Sø, the second lake, you'll pass the bronze statue of Nilen and then, on the opposite side of the road, Tiberen. Cast from Roman marble originals dating back to the 1st century, the men represent the rivers Nile and Tiber.

Head along the banks of the third lake, Sortedams Sø. To the right are the picturesque Kartoffelraekkerne (Potato Row Houses). Towards the end of the third lake the water is concealed by construction: it's part of the Cityringen Metro expansion, due for completion in 2019. Cut across the temporary pedestrian bridge and head back south. The western edge of the lakes has tunnels under the major intersections; watch for these paths to your right. The road veers from the path for the stretch along Sankt Jørgens Sø. This tranquil change offers uninterrupted views of stately residences and suburban gardens. Finish your lap at the starting point.

Walks
—— Find your own Copenhagen

While the bicycle deservedly gets a lot of play in Copenhagen, the flat topography, wide streets and easy-to-navigate layout also lend themselves to exploration by foot (not least because it's much easier to duck into the endless boutiques and cafés). The city may be compact but a flurry of development and regeneration over the past 10 years has resulted in districts with different characters and attractions. Here are five urban walks through our favourite ones.

NEIGHBOURHOOD 01

Islands Brygge
Quayside revitalised

South of the city centre, Islands Brygge (literally "Iceland's Quay") was at the heart of trade between Denmark and Iceland from the late 1800s to the mid-20th century. This sudden boom in industry saw five- to six-storey residential blocks rapidly erected with little pause for liveability or aesthetics. Two-bedroom apartments were often occupied by multiple working-class families, and the streetscape had little greenery or ornamentation. Even as you walk through the neighbourhood today, this lack of decorative character is still apparent in comparison to the more modern development to the neighbourhood's north.

Trade waned in the 1950s and the area became a wasteland until residents lobbied local government to redevelop it in the 1990s. Now the 2km-long stretch along the harbour is a major thoroughfare for commuters; in summer the Bjarke Ingels-designed decks of the Harbour Baths heave with sunseekers.

But the real pull of the neighbourhood lies back from the water in the once-empty warehouses and decommissioned workshops. In the past decade these spaces have become a magnet for carpenters, potters and artists, and brands such as Studio Arhoj and Københavns Møbelsnedkeri now have their studios here. This flourishing community of creatives and makers is worth the trip across the Langebro.

Harbourside tour
Islands Brygge walk

Kickstart your walk with an espresso at the homely corner café ❶ *Wulff + Konstali Food Shop*. Exit and head southwest to the end of Isafjordsgade. Across the junction sits the striking four-storey office of technology consultancy ❷ *Kombit*. Designed in 2008 by Danielsen Architecture, the floor-to-ceiling glass façade flanked by copper panelling is an anomaly among the older neighbouring blocks.

Address book

01 Wulff + Konstali
Food Shop
10 Isafjordsgade
+45 3254 8181
wogk.dk

02 Kombit
8 Halfdansgade
danielsenarch.com

03 Ballonparken
73 Artillerivej

04 Faste Batteri
8 Ørestads Boulevard
kolonihave.nu

05 Studio Arhoj
8M Kigkurren
+45 2989 5800
arhoj.com

06 The Shop of the New
14 Sturlasgade
+45 3331 3030
Shopofthenew.com

07 Monika Petersen
Art Prints
7 Gunløgsgade
+45 2092 2852
monikapetersen.com

08 Antik Keramik
8 Isafjordsgade
+45 4062 3619

09 Kirkegaards Antikvariat
25 Islands Brygge
+45 2447 7714
kirkegaardsantikvariat.dk

10 GoBoat
10 Islands Brygge
+45 4026 1025
goboat.dk

11 Dvaele
2 Reykjaviksgade
+45 4277 0193
dvaele.dk

12 Alimentari
19C Njalsgade, 2300
+45 2674 6544
alimentari.dk

Head left along Halfdansgade and cross Artillerivej to the Amagerfaelled parkland. The red wooden homes at the northern border of the park once housed military personnel who worked at ③ *Ballonparken* (Balloon Park), testing the firing range of cannons with the help of hot-air balloons targets. The wooden hangar used to store the balloons still stands, and is now a horse-riding arena.

Turn left down the gravel path, winding east through Amagerfaelled to reach ④ *Faste Batteri*. This community was founded in 1940 as part of a Kolonihave (colony garden). Families bought these cheap properties to live closer to nature in summer but still within city limits. Head back west through the park along the main footpath toward Artillerivej. As you exit take a right, then turn left down Kigkurren and enter through the arch at number 6-8. Follow the neon sign of ⑤ *Studio Arhoj* into the rear block and up one flight of stairs. Here in the studio-cum-shop you can watch the potters throw vases and mugs and leave with your own original.

Back out on Kigkurren continue left until it changes into Sturlasgade and enter through the industrial block opposite the stables to visit ⑥ *The Shop of the New*. It stocks functional oak chairs and shelves from the Københavns Møbelsnedkeri joinery opposite. Back on the street, double back and loop round behind the stables, north down Snorresgade. Right on Gunløgsgade is ⑦ *Monika Petersen Art Prints*. Petersen's prints pair her affinity to detail with Danish simplicity.

Getting there
———
The M1 line on the Metro, running from Frederiksberg and Norreport stops at Islands Brygge Station, which is a seven-minute walk from the starting point. Alternatively, the 250S bus from the Tivoli stops opposite Wulff + Konstali Food Shop.

Next take a left on Isafjordsgade and stop in at ⑧ *Antik Keramik* to browse through Jens Bak Rasmussen's collection of vintage Royal Copenhagen ceramics, Lego sets from the 1950s and '60s and rare wooden toys. Turn left along Egilsgade, then left again to reach bookshop ⑨ *Kirkegaards Antikvariat*. Here you can thumb through a curious collection of photography, architecture and design books and magazines.

Head back the way you came along Islands Brygge. If the weather's good hire a solar-powered motor boat from ⑩ *GoBoat*. You don't need experience; just stock up at the on-site deli then head out. Back on shore, cross the park to walk up Vestmannagade passing artist-run homeware shop Formverk on the corner. Go right on Thorshavnsgade; on the next corner is gallery and design shop ⑪ *Dvaele*, run by artists Maria-Louise Andkaer and Paw Grabowski. To end your tour, head southeast along Klaksvigsgade then take the stairs up past Founders House to arrive at ⑫ *Alimentari* for an Italian feast.

NEIGHBOURHOOD 02
Christianshavn
Maritime marvel

With its tree-lined canals, industrial warehouses and (in)famous hippie commune, it's hard to believe Christianshavn is just a short stroll from the city centre. It was built on the eastern coast – across the harbour from Christiansborg Palace and the Danish stock exchange – between 1618 and 1623 by Christian IV, king of Denmark during the first half of the 17th century. A merchant and fortress town, its primary purpose was to house the workers building Denmark's navy. By 1674, however, it was incorporated into its older – and larger – sibling.

Today the area is largely residential, with an Amsterdam-like feel (thanks to its canals and, perhaps, Freetown Christiania's green-light district). It's a healthy mix of 18th-century warehouses and modern Scandinavian design, its old brick buildings turned into sought-after lofts and apartments. The area is rife with creative businesses, Instagram-worthy cafés and independent shops and boutiques. Unsurprisingly, Christianshavn has become a magnet for the city's cool characters – young and old, bohemian and tailored – who have come to think of it as Copenhagen's laidback heart. Stroll along its canals and cobbled streets – home to antique sailing boats and handsome colour-washed houses – and you'll soon see why. All it takes is a hint of sunshine for the crowds to descend, beer in hand, onto the neighbourhood's piers.

Creativity tour
Christianshavn walk

Start on the left-hand side of Knippelsbro Bridge, heading away from the city centre towards Christianshavn. When you reach dry land continue straight on Torvegade and before long you'll see ❶ *Munk*, a two-storey design shop that sells everything from carpets to clocks.

Once your design needs are satisfied nip across Torvegade and turn right down Wildersgarde,

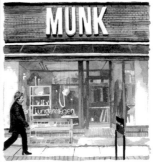

a pretty cobbled street that's quieter than the main drag. Stroll to the end – signalled by one of Christianshavn's many canals – and follow the block around to the left onto Overgaden Neden Vandet. Cross back over Torvegade and continue along the canal on Overgaden Oven Vandet until you reach Sankt Annae Gade. Turn right, crossing the canal, and ahead you'll soon see the ❷ *Church of Our Saviour*. This baroque beauty is worth a pit-stop, if only to climb its twisting black-and-gold spire.

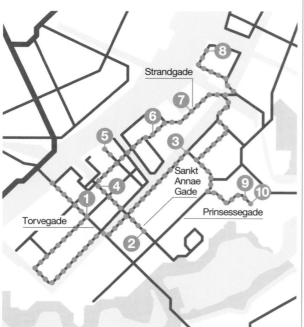

Getting there

It's just a short walk from Stroget to the starting point on Knippel Bridge if you want to avoid public transport. Alternatively, the M1 and M2 lines of the metro stop at Kongens Nytorv – as does bus route S – which is a 10-minute walk.

After soaking up the view, exit on the corner of Sankt Annae Gade and Prinsessegade, turning left and walking along the latter. Cross Bådsmandsstraede and continue past a fabulously graffitied building and the entrance to Freetown Christiania on your right; don't stop, you'll return here later. When Prinsessegade forks, go left and then turn left again onto Brobergsgade. You can refuel at the end at ③ *Parterre*, a small family-run café with a simple menu.

When you've had your fill head left along Overgaden Oven Vandet, crossing the first bridge you come to on your right. Continue straight along Sankt Annae Gade, crossing Wildersgade, to find ④ *Sweet Treat* on your right, a cosy spot for coffee or (you guessed it) something sugary. Turn right as you leave and then right again onto Strandgade; a left onto Bådmandsstraede gets you to the ⑤ *Dansk Arkitektur Centre (see page 118)*. If you have time, see an exhibition; if not, take a turn around the bookshop.

Return to Strandgade and continue northeast, crossing

Wildersbro Bridge and following the street. Pop into ⑥ *Edition Copenhagen*, a lithographic workshop and gallery. Then, as Strandgade bends to the right it forks again; veer left. ⑦ *North Atlantic House* will be on your left. This 16th-century warehouse was the centre of shipping traffic between Denmark and the north Atlantic, and you can learn about the district's maritime history.

Turn left from here back on Strandgade, and follow it round onto the Butterfly 3-Way Bridge. At the junction in the middle, take the left-hand bridge to Paper Island. Turn left and follow the signs to ⑧ *Copenhagen Street Food (see page 35)* for a nibble or a tipple.

Hop off the island via the same bridge but this time go left over its third arm. Follow the path to the right along the canal, turn left down Bodenhoffs Plads and right onto Andreas Bjørns Gade. At the end of the block turn left and then right, and follow Prinsessegade. About 100 metres on the left is the entrance to Freetown Christiania, between two totem poles.

The cannabis-tolerant green-light district is straight ahead but if you want to aim for a different destination, swing to the left and turn left again before the Christiania Jazz Club. Take a right turn and before long you'll come to ⑨ *Kvindesmedien*, a delightfully industrial workshop and gallery run by women metalsmiths.

Along the path is your final stop: ⑩ *Christiania Cykler* sells and rents all sorts of bikes. Choose one and continue on wheels, or head through the greenery and people-watch the rest of the day away.

Address book

01 Munk
25 Torvegade
+45 3336 5554
munkshop.dk
02 Church of Our Saviour
29 Sankt Annae Gade
03 Parterre
90 Overgaden
Oven Vandet
04 Sweet Treat
3A Sankt Annae Gade
+45 3295 4115
sweettreat.dk
05 Dansk Arkitektur Centre
27B Strandgade
+45 3257 1930
dac.dk
06 Edition Copenhagen
66 Strandgade
+45 3254 3311
editioncopenhagen.com
07 North Atlantic House
91 Strandgade
+45 3283 3700
nordatlantens.dk
08 Copenhagen Street Food
14 Transgravsvej
Paper Island
copenhagenstreetfood.dk
09 Kvindesmedien
83 Maelkevejen
+45 3257 7658
kvindesmedien.dk
10 Christiania Cykler
91 Fabriksområdet
+45 3295 4520
christianiacykler.dk

NEIGHBOURHOOD 03

City Centre
Copenhagen's heart

The boundaries of Indre By, Copenhagen's inner-city district, once marked those of the entire town. King Christian IV expanded the city with the building of bridges, new districts and grand palaces but ultimately it was fire and water that would define the capital.

Fire shaped the city in the early and late 18th century. One, starting in Vesterport in 1728, destroyed more than 1,500 buildings, while a second that broke out in the dockyards of Gammelholm in 1795 brought further devastation. Thanks to these blazes, little remains of medieval and renaissance Copenhagen; much of its housing dates from the 18th and 19th centuries. The legacy of the fires is still visible: modern buildings have curved corners for hoses to wrap round them with no loss of water pressure.

Water is abundant here – about half the city borders the Øresund Strait – and much development has occured along the harbour in recent years. This walk will take you past some of the highlights, including the Royal Danish Playhouse, which was designed by Lundgaard & Tranberg and opened in 2008. Just across the water sits Henning Larsen's striking 14-storey Opera House (*see page 104*), which opened in 2005. The architect was famously disappointed with the final result; today it's a city landmark and much loved by concert audiences.

Sightseeing tour
City Centre walk

Start off at ❶ *Café Atelier September* with coffee and a fresh produce-driven meal (try the avocado on rye). Exit, turn right and walk a little more than a block to ❷ *Rosenborg Castle*. The Dutch renaissance-style castle was built by King Christian IV in the early 17th century and a wander through its grandly decorated rooms is well worth the price of admission (the Crown Jewels are also housed here).

Head back to the south corner of the park and cross to walk down Møntergade. At the corner of Gammel Mønt is a red house with a gable dormer, an example of an *ildebrandshuse* townhouse built following the fire of 1728. Turn right on to Vognmagergade. After a block and a half you'll see the stone entrance to the ❸ *KVUC building*. The lobby of the adult education centre has one of the city's five paternoster lifts, a perpetually moving open lift that dates back to 1913 (unsurprisingly, they fell out of favour due to safety concerns). After you've gone for a spin, head northwest on Vognmagergade. Turn left when you reach Landemaerket. Walk a few minutes to the ❹ *Round Tower* (Rundetårn), King Christian IV's former astronomy observatory. The much-repeated rumour is that Peter the Great rode his horse to the top in 1716, his wife, Catherine I, following behind in a carriage.

See the view from the top, then head down to Krystalgade and ❺ *Another Nué*, a boutique that stocks a quality mix of Danish and international designers. Across the

Getting there

Hotels within the City Centre
are a short walk from the
starting point. The Kongens
Nytorv Metro stop that is
serviced by the M1 and M2
lines is a five-minute walk
away. Numerous buses
also run from the outer
suburbs into the city centre.

Address book

01 Café Atelier September
30 Gothersgade
cafeatelierseptember.com
02 Rosenborg Castle
4A Øster Voldgade
+45 3315 3286
03 KVUC building
8 Vognmagergade
+45 8232 6600
04 Round Tower
52A Købmagergade
+45 3373 0373
rundetaarn.dk/en
05 Another Nué
3 Krystalgade
+45 3312 3302
nuecph.com
06 AC Perch's Thehandel
5 Kronprinsensgade
+45 3315 3562
perchs.dk
07 Hotel d'Angleterre
34 Kongens Nytorv
+45 3312 0095
dangleterre.com
08 Nyhavn
Kongens Nytorv to
Havnepromenade
09 Royal Danish Playhouse
36 Sankt Annae Plads
+45 3369 6969
kglteater.dk
10 Amalienborg
5 Amalienborg Slotsplads
+45 3312 2186

road you'll also find Henrik Vibskov,
arguably Copenhagen's most high-
profile fashion designer.

Double back and turn right at
the Rundetårn onto Købmagergade.
At Kronprinsensgade, turn left.
A few doors down you'll see
❻ *AC Perch's Thehandel*, a tea
shop that dates back to 1835. On
the floor above is a tea room with
more than 150 types of leaf tea, as
well as finger sandwiches, petits
fours and scones.

Exit left and continue straight
onto Ny Østergade. Turn right,
then left at Hovedvagtsgade. At the
intersection, right on the corner, is
❼ *Hotel d'Angleterre*, the city's most
storied accommodation for visitors
(*see page 22*). For some years during
the 1860s the city's most famous
literary son (admittedly adopted),
Hans Christian Andersen, lived in
rooms overlooking Kongens Nytorv
across the road.

To see another of the writer's
famous haunts walk around
Kongens Nytorv, with the theatre
buildings on your right. When you
hit the canal you'll see the café
umbrellas and brightly painted
buildings of what is perhaps
the city's most well-known site:
❽ *Nyhavn*. It was once the sordid
underbelly of the city but the
prostitutes and sailors have long
been replaced by camera-toting
tourists. Accordingly it can be
hard to find a seat and the beer is
hideously overpriced, so make like
the locals: buy drinks from a nearby
shop then hunker down where you
can; street drinking is legal here.

Stay on the left of the canal
and when you reach the harbour
you'll see one of the shiniest
additions to the city, the ❾ *Royal
Danish Playhouse*. Follow the
boardwalk around the building
near the harbour; come off it and
cross the open ground to Larsens
Plads, turning right to pass the
Copenhagen Admiral Hotel, dating
back to 1787. Follow the water to
Amalie Garden, turn left at the
water feature and walk to the grand
buildings ahead – this is
❿ *Amalienborg*, home of the Danish
royal family. A flag will be flying when
Queen Margrethe II or Crown Prince
Frederik and his Australian-born wife,
Crown Princess Mary, are in residence.

NEIGHBOURHOOD 04
Vesterbro
Vice turns nice

A livestock-trading district dating back to the 1600s, Vesterbro acquired a more scurrilous aspect in later years as home to the city's red-light district. Istedgade in particular – running from Copenhagen Central to Enghave Plads – was known as a hotbed of sex, drugs and porn. However, extensive renovation, along with an influx of students and creatives, has given the area a revitalising shot in the arm. It's still a very different prospect from the more touristy City Centre; down some side streets, traditional working-men's bars are still commonplace and, near Enghave Plads, an old workers' club building designed by Vilhelm Lauritzen has become one of the city's most rambunctious nightspots, Vega (*see page 100*). That said, this is now a vibrant, family-friendly area with plenty of spots to grab a quality coffee or a meal, and an altogether more salubrious brand of nightlife.

While Istedgade is home to many independent fashion and design retailers, cafés and bars, and well worth a meander, Vesterbro's main drawcard is undoubtedly Kødbyen, the city's former meatpacking district. Its three areas – White, Brown and Grey – were named for the predominant colours of their buildings; heritage-listed structures now colonised by restaurants, art galleries, makers, designers, pubs and clubs (although you'll still see the odd fishmonger or butcher carrying their wares through the area).

Heritage appreciation
Vesterbro walk

This walk starts with a wander around the Carlsberg Brewery. It was founded in 1847 by Jacob Christian Jacobsen, who introduced Bavarian-style lager to Denmark. The collection of incongruous buildings – including the striking quartet of swastika-bearing elephants – certainly look as if they were dreamt up by someone with a few under their belt.

Head down Ny Carlsberg Vej, passing below the **1** *Elephant Gate*, which was built in 1901 and designed by architect Vilhelm Dahlerup. Beer enthusiasts can peel off right down Olivia Hansens Gade (follow the signs) to visit the brewery and sample the Jacobsen craft beers still produced on-site (the main production plant is now based in Fredericia). You'll notice plenty of building work as the site is being transformed into a residential and entertainment hub.

Continue down Ny Carlsberg Vej to Vesterfaelledvej and turn left. Enter **2** *Galleri Nicolai Wallner*, one of the city's largest contemporary art spaces that hosts a thought-provoking roster of artists.

Walk back to the intersection of Ny Carlsberg Vej and turn left, crossing the road and walking along the edge of Enghave Park. When you reach the intersection of Enghavevej, cross and walk down Enghave Plads. In a few minutes you'll reach **3** *Bageriet Brød*, a bakery where all the organic treats sold are made in the stone oven in the back of the shop. Pick up a pastry and continue on.

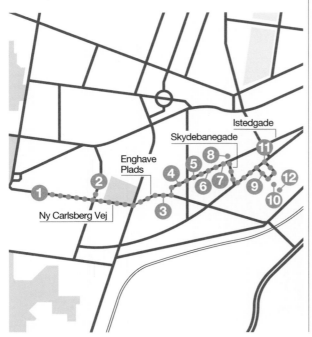

Getting there

A free bus runs every hour to the Carlsberg Brewery (11.00 to 17.00, from March to September) from outside the Royal Hotel at 6 Vesterbrogade, near Central Station. The area is also serviced by the 18 and 26 buses. The Bycyklen hub is at the intersection of Enghavevej and Enghaveparken.

You'll see a road leading off to the left; take this to reach Istedgade, a formerly dicey street that is now one of the best stretches of independent retailers in the city. Turn right and walk two blocks to ④ *Café Bang & Jensen*, a café and bar housed in a former pharmacy. The brunch here is top notch.

The first retail port of call is ⑤ *Kyoto*, which stocks a solid mix of street-smart men's and women's fashion and footwear. Cross Saxogade and a few doors down on your left-hand side you'll see ⑥ *Es*, a tiny sliver of a shop with a small but interesting range of womenswear.

Continue on for another block. On your left you'll come across ⑦ *Dansk Made for Rooms* (*see page 54*), Malene Sofie and Ma-lou Westendahl's excellent homeware store for lighting, ceramics, textiles and furniture.

When you're done perusing, step outside and turn left down the side street. You'll see the red-brick ⑧ *Shooting Range Wall*. Through its opening there's a children's slide in the shape of a parrot, a nod to the

original use of this area. Marksmen used to aim at a wooden parrot on a pole (bullet holes can be seen in the top of the wall) and it's where the Danish term "shooting the parrot" as an expression of good luck originates.

Head back the way you came and cross Istedgade, continuing straight on. When you reach Sønder Boulevard, turn left and continue for two blocks until you see a path leading right towards the distinctive white-and-blue façade of the city's hip entertainment hotspot, the Meatpacking District. If you're in need of a coffee, pop into the tiny but terrific ⑨ *Prolog Coffee Bar*, (*see page 43*) on Høkerboderne. The area is also home to a number of art galleries. A couple of doors down you can see what's on at ⑩ *Gallery Poulsen*, a contemporary-art space that represents mostly US artists.

To finish off the walk we recommend some shared plates at ⑪ *Paté Paté*, or one of the other restaurants in our food section (*see pages 31 – 34*). Top things off with a drink at the lively ⑫ *Noho Bar*.

Address book

01 Elephant Gate
Gamle Carlsberg Vej
+45 3327 1282
visitcarlsberg.com

02 Galleri Nicolai Wallner
68 Ny Carlsberg Vej
+45 3257 0970
nicolaiwallner.com

03 Bageriet Brød
7 Enghave Plads
+45 3322 8007

04 Café Bang & Jensen
130 Istedgade
+45 3325 5318

05 Kyoto
95 Istedgade
+45 3331 6636
kyoto.dk

06 Es
110 Istedgade
+45 3322 4829
es-es.dk

07 Dansk Made for Rooms
80 Istedgade
+45 3218 0255
danskmadeforrooms.dk

08 Shooting Range Wall
74 Istedgade

09 Prolog Coffee Bar
16 Høkerboderne
+45 3125 5675

10 Gallery Poulsen
24 Flaesketorvet
+45 3333 9396
gallerypoulsen.com

11 Paté Paté
1 Slagterboderne
+45 3969 5557
patepate.dk

12 Noho Bar
26-28 Flaesketorvet
+45 7199 5990
noho.bar

NEIGHBOURHOOD 05
Nørrebro
Copenhagen's hot spot

Nørrebro in the 18th century consisted of little more than countryside: small settlements existing outside the ramparts of Copenhagen. It was only when an overcrowding crisis hit the city in 1852 that the district was brought within the city limits, triggering building work and exploding the population by the turn of the 20th century.

Like Vesterbro, the area was characterised by working-class families in small homes and by the 1970s Nørrebro had a reputation as one of the city's less appealing neighbourhoods.

With redevelopment came the Nørrebro we know today, a multicultural district that enjoys larger residences, more green spaces and a rich social landscape. Sankt Hans Torv is the heart of the area but Jaegersborggade has become a destination in its own right. Many are drawn by its reputation as one of the best places in the city to find coffee.

The district's main drag, Nørrebrogade, is the place to shop, with a weekend flea market (from March to October) on top of the regular retail options. There are retro bargains to be found on Blågårdsgade and Elmegade, from vintage clothes to classic vinyl. Nørrebrogade will also take you past the literal dead centre of town: the Assistens Kirkegård, a popular chillout area for locals, is the final resting place of Hans Christian Andersen.

Cultural safari
Nørrebro walk

To start this walk, head to the banks of the peaceful Peblinge Lake, a short hop from the busy train station of Nørreport. Settle down for some bacon-laden brunch on historical café **1** *Kaffesalonen's* floating pontoon. The 1930s venue has a charmingly old-school feel, helped by the colourful pedalos parked by the deck (which are also for hire). Once your feet are back on land, head down the leafy backstreets by the lake until you reach Åboulevard. Here, squeezed between two red-brick buildings, you'll find a lesser-known architectural wonder: **2** *Bethlehem Church*. With its dramatic stepped gable, Nørrebro's tall parish church is similar in style to the expressionist Grundtvig's Church (both were designed by eminent architect Kaare Klint) but much easier to reach from the city centre.

When a spot of shopping is in order, turn right onto Blågårdsgade: there's plenty to choose from but take your time at **3** *Topskat*, a compact treasure-trove of exceptional secondhand furniture and design trinkets. Proceed through the intersection with the neighbourhood's main artery – Nørrebrogade – and veer right to head up Ravnsborggade with its impressive mural of a cycling woman, created by Finnish-Danish artist Seppo Mattinen. If it's already past midday don't forget to stock up on some of the excellent international labels lining the shelves of wine shop **4** *Vintro*. **5** *Café Gavlen*, on the corner with Sankt Hans Gade, makes the

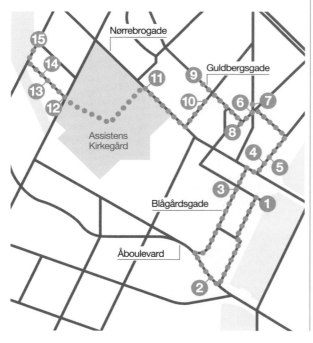

Nørrebrogade

Guldbergsgade

15
14
13
11
9
12
10
6
7
8
4
5
3
1

Assistens
Kirkegård

Blågårdsgade

Åboulevard

2

Address book

01 **Kaffesalonen**
6 Peblinge Dossering
+45 3535 1219
kaffesalonen.com

02 **Bethlehem Church**
8 Åboulevard
+45 3539 7703
bethlehemskirken.dk

03 **Topskat**
13 Blågårdsgade
butiktopskat.dk

04 **Vintro**
5 Ravnsborggade
+45 5122 0002
vintrovin.dk

05 **Café Gavlen**
1 Ryesgade
+45 3537 0237
gavlen.dk

06 **Sankt Hans Torv**

07 **Mr Larkin**
1 Nørre Allé
mrlarkin.net

08 **Hooha**
14 Elmegade
+45 3537 6037
hooha.dk

09 **Mirabelle**
29 Guldbergsgade
+45 3535 4724
mirabelle-bakery.dk

10 **Jewish Cemetery**
12 Møllegade

11 **Accord Nørrebro**
90 Nørrebrogade
+45 7015 1617
accord.dk

12 **Den Sidste Dråbe**
6 Jaegersborggade
+45 2982 9637

13 **Kaktus København**
35 Jaegersborggade
+45 2341 5918
kaktuskbh.dk

14 **Manfreds**
40 Jaegersborggade
+45 3696 6593
manfreds.dk

15 **Mikkeller & Friends**
35 Stefansgade
+45 3583 1020
mikkeller.dk

Getting there

Sat between Frederiksberg and Østerbro, Nørrebro is walking distance from both. While the closest metro station is Nørreport on the other side of the lakes, buses 5A and 350S make for easy access to the neighbourhood's main thoroughfare, Nørrebrogade.

best lattes in the area: grab one for a mid-walk perk-up before heading towards ⑥ *Sankt Hans Torv*. Often dubbed the neighbourhood's centre for nightlife, this square is just as lovely during the day, with its relaxed cafés and striking granite sculpture by Jørgen Haugen Sørensen. Our favourite spot here, though, is womenswear shop ⑦ *Mr Larkin*: owner Casey Larkin Blond showcases labels from Denmark and beyond, as well as her own brand of boxy, minimal clothing. The small alleys of Elmegade and Birkegade are worth perusing for shoes and accessories: to get your fill of trainers, diminutive but well-stocked ⑧ *Hooha* is your best bet.

By now tummies will be rumbling so skip down Guldbergsgade to get to ⑨ *Mirabelle*. Grab a thin steel chair in this cosy organic bakery and enjoy a spinach, egg and pancetta salad with a generous slice of sourdough. A little back-tracking won't hurt so amble around one of Nørrebro's best-kept secrets: at the corner of Møllegade is the entrance to the ⑩ *Jewish Cemetery*, a smaller, quieter but

no less fascinating counterpart to nearby Assistens Kirkegård. Don't be scared to double up on atmospheric graveyards: head to the latter via the entrance in front of the bright yellow, 1960s-inspired sign of music shop ⑪ *Accord Nørrebro* (but not before popping in to pick up some Danish tunes on vinyl). Proceed until you get to a pathway lined by poplars: turn right and continue until you exit onto Nørrebro's retail heaven Jaeggersborggade. Every other shop is worthy of a lengthy wander but don't skip small-batch distiller ⑫ *Den Sidste Dråbe's* craft vodka. And make a point of stopping at ⑬ *Kaktus København*, Copenhagen's cutest succulent-only plant shop, where cacti from miniature to desert-sized always catch the attention. When it's time to sit down for a meal, opt for ⑭ *Manfreds*: at this tiny corner-venue (sister restaurant to the fancier Relae, *see page 28*) small plates come accompanied by tasty natural wines. To conclude the day, grab a glass of spiced ale at ⑮ *Mikkeller & Friends*: you've surely earned it.

Resources
—— Inside knowledge

By now you've noted the best places to grab a bite or a brew, the top shops for everything from clothes to books and all the cultural and artistic sights and sounds you can possibly squeeze into a trip to Copenhagen. Here's where you can pick up some useful words and phrases, get to grips with public transport and load up on ideas for activities come rain or shine. We've even whipped up a Copenhagen-centric playlist for you to enjoy while you plan your visit or wander the city.

Transport
Get around town

01 **Bicycle:** There are extensive cycle routes and tons of shops to hire bikes from (many hotels also lend them). The Bycyklen public bikes can be found at hubs throughout the city and have built-in GPS and touch-screen maps.
bycyklen.dk

02 **City Pass:** There are nine public transport zones but you'll probably only travel in three, including when getting to and from the airport. City Pass covers bus, Metro and the train and costs DKK80 (€11) for the day or DKK200 (€27) for three days for an adult. Another good value option is the Copenhagen Card which combines public transport with access to 73 museums and attractions (a 72-hour card costs €85).
citypass.dk;
copenhagencard.com

03 **Bus:** These red-and-yellow vehicles run on central routes every three to seven minutes in rush hour (07.00 to 09.00 and 15.30 to 17.30) or every 10 minutes. They also operate all night, 365 days a year.
dinoffentligetransport.dk

04 **Metro:** The M1 and M2 lines run from Nørreport to Kongens Nytorv and Christianshavn. The M2 links to the airport.
intl.m.dk

05 **Taxi and car:** Only hire a car if you must. Parking is expensive and driving in the city centre discouraged. Taxis are easily hailed.

06 **Waterbus:** These blue-and-yellow shuttle boats run along and across the harbourfront and are covered by the City Pass. In summer a series of hop-on, hop-off boat tours are operated by Strömma.
rejseplanen.dk
stromma.dk

07 **Trains:** The S-tog trains run between 05.00 and 00.30 on weekdays and all night on Fridays and Saturdays.
dsb.dk/en

Vocabulary
Local lingo

Danish is a challenging language (luckily most Danes speak excellent English) but here are some handy words:

01 **Hello:** Hej
02 **Goodbye:** hej hej
03 **Thank you:** tak
04 **Cheers:** skål
05 **Spis lige brød:** calm down
06 **Det var hyggeligt:** cheers for the good times
07 **Tak for kaffe:** no way/really?!

Soundtrack to the city
Five top tunes

From nostalgia-soaked throwbacks and whimsical electronica to the most bubble-gum pop song *ever* created, our Copenhagen playlist is as varied as the city itself.

01 **Danny Kaye, 'Wonderful Copenhagen':** Plucked from the 1952 musical *Hans Christian Andersen*, this is possibly the most famous song about the city

02 **The Raveonettes 'Love in a Trashcan':** The hip indie-rock darlings employ their 1950s guitar-driven style to great effect in this offbeat ditty about misguided romance.

03 **Aqua, 'Barbie Girl':** There are Danes who feel that the perennial popularity of this super-kitsch Scandi pop export is a nightmare that won't end but there's no denying it's super catchy.

04 **Trentemøller, 'Take Me Into Your Skin':** The debut album from this Copenhagen-based electronic musician is packed with atmospheric tunes such as this that manage to simultaneously soothe, haunt and elevate.

05 **Efterklang, 'Modern Drift':** Gentle indie rock, orchestral elements and an electronic flavour combine in this track by the well-loved Danish trio.

Best events
What to see

01 CPH:Dox, various venues: Documentary movies are the focus here, with more than 200 screenings. *March, cphdox.dk*

02 Ølfestival, Lokomotivvaerkstedet: Learn about – and sample – more than 800 varieties of beer in a three-day festival. *May, ale.dk*

03 Distortion Festival, various venues: This event features street parties and music, from metal and house to trip hop and more. *June, cphdistortion.dk*

04 Sankt Hans Aften, nationwide: Danes mark the height of summer (St John's Eve) with food, drink and bonfires, on which the effigies of witches are burned. *23 June*

05 Roskilde Festival, Roskilde: North Europe's largest music festival boasts international headline acts, street art and culture. *June & July, roskilde-festival.dk*

06 Copenhagen Jazz Festival, various venues: This 10-day celebration of live music draws 250,000 jazz-lovers to the city every year. *July, jazz.dk*

07 Copenhagen Cooking and Food Festival, various venues: The Meatpacking District comes alive with more than 300 events. *August, copenhagen cooking.com*

08 Chart Art Fair, Kunsthal Charlottenborg: Leading galleries and creatives showcase the best of Nordic art and design. *August, chartartfair.com*

09 Art Copenhagen, Bella Center: A festival of all things artistic, with dozens of galleries participating. *August, artcopenhagen.dk*

10 CPH Pix, various venues: Copenhagen's annual festival of film. *October & November, cphpix.dk*

Sunny days
The great outdoors

01 Tivoli Gardens, City Centre: Tivoli isn't just for tourists; it attracts Danes of all ages throughout the year. On a sunny day make the most of the lush surroundings with a stroll around the tulip lawn followed by a picnic while watching an outdoor film. Every day during the summer season there is a different open-air concert – from jazz to folk, classical to pop – and on Fridays at 22.00, international rock stars take to the stage. *tivoli.dk*

02 Relax in a cemetery: When the sun comes out be sure to make the most of Copenhagen's green spaces – specifically the city's graveyards, which are used as much by the living as by the dead. Assistens Kirkegård in Nørrebro is the most popular and home to the headstones of Hans Christian Andersen, Søren Kierkegaard and other celebrated Danes. Take a stroll along its paths and join the residents sunbathing and socialising among the rhododendron bushes and picturesque tombs. *assistens.dk*

03 See the city by boat: It may seem cheesy but hopping on board a boat can be one of the most enjoyable and effective ways to get to grips with the city, particularly its ever-evolving harbour and the historic canals of Christianshavn. Tour boats depart regularly from Nyhavn and Gammel Strand – and the latter tour is free with a Copenhagen Card. Or, if you'd prefer to be the captain of your own ship, you can choose to rent a vessel yourself. Companies such as GoBoat don't even require you to have a boating licence. *stromma.dk; goboat.dk*

Rainy days
Weather-proof activities

01 Explore a museum: Culture vultures won't be disappointed come the rain: Copenhagen has an array of internationally renowned museums in which to take refuge. For something quintessentially Danish make a dash for Designmuseum Danmark, which invites you to walk along a timeline of the country's talented designers. If you're in the mood for something a little more kooky, the experimental artists showing at Den Frie Centre of Contemporary Art never fail to amaze. *designmuseum.dk; denfrie.dk*

02 Visit a culture house: A meeting place for the city's creatives and for people of all ages, Copenhagen's culture houses invite you to mingle with both neighbours and strangers. Best described as a kind of community centre, they're the place to enjoy a range of activities, from yoga classes to ceramic workshops and beer brewing. Huset-KBH is Denmark's largest culture house, hosting more than 1,400 events a year. *huset-kbh.dk*

03 Pick a palace: The city is dotted with palaces and castles that invite the public in to view royal regalia and other items of monarchic significance. Admire the Danish Crown Jewels in the renaissance Rosenborg Castle or head to Christiansborg Palace, the seat of the Danish government, to tour the Royal Reception Rooms. Don't miss the city's changing of the Royal Guard; every day around 11.30 the bearskin-topped infantrymen march from Rosenborg Castle to the Amalienborg Palace. *kongernessamling.dk*

About Monocle
—— Step inside

London HQ

Our editorial office is in Marylebone

In 2007, Monocle was launched as a monthly magazine briefing on global affairs, business, culture, design and much more. We believed there was a globally minded audience of readers who were hungry for opportunities and experiences beyond their national borders.

Today Monocle is a complete media brand with print, audio and online elements – not to mention our expanding network of shops and cafés. Besides our London HQ we have seven international bureaux in New York, Toronto, Istanbul, Singapore, Tokyo, Zürich and Hong Kong. We continue to grow and flourish and at our core is the simple belief that there will always be a place for a print brand that is committed to telling fresh stories and sending photographers on assignments. It's also a case of knowing that our success is all down to the readers, advertisers and collaborators who have supported us along the way.

❶
International bureaux
Boots on the ground

We have an HQ in London and call upon firsthand reports from our contributors in more than 35 cities around the world. We also have seven international bureaux. For this travel guide, MONOCLE reporters Amy Richardson, Mikaela Aitken, Chloë Ashby and Chiara Rimella jumped on their bicycles and got pedalling to explore all that Copenhagen has to offer. They also called on the assistance of writers in the city, including our correspondent Michael Booth, to ensure we have covered the very best in retail, food, hospitality and entertainment. The aim is to make you, the reader, feel like a local.

❷
Online
Digital delivery

We have a dynamic website: *monocle.com*. As well as being the place to hear our radio station, Monocle 24, the site presents our films, which are beautifully shot and edited by our in-house team and provide a fresh perspective on our stories. Check out the films celebrating the cities that make up our Travel Guide Series before you explore the rest of the site.

❸
Retail and cafés
Food for thought

Via our shops in Hong Kong, Toronto, New York, Tokyo, London and Singapore we sell products that cater to our readers' tastes and are produced in collaboration with brands we believe in. We also have cafés in Tokyo and London. And if you are in the UK capital, visit the Kioskafé in Paddington, which combines good coffee and great reads.

❹
Print
Committed to the page

MONOCLE is published 10 times a year. We have stayed loyal to our belief in quality print with two extra seasonal publications: THE FORECAST, packed with key insights into the year ahead, and THE ESCAPIST, our summer travel-minded magazine. To sign up visit *monocle.com/subscribe*. Since 2013 we have also been publishing books, like this one, in partnership with Gestalten.

❺
Radio
Sound approach

Monocle 24 is our round-the-clock radio station that was launched in 2011. It delivers global news and shows covering foreign affairs, urbanism, business, culture, food and drink, design and print media. When you find yourself in Denmark, tune into *The Urbanist* to see which other cities strive to be as liveable as Copenhagen. We also have a playlist to accompany you day and night, regularly assisted by live band sessions that are hosted at our Midori House headquarters in London. You can listen live or download any of our shows from *monocle.com*, iTunes or SoundCloud.

Join the club

01
Subscribe to Monocle
A subscription is a simple way to make sure you never miss a copy and enjoy many additional benefits.

02
Read every issue published
Our subscribers have exclusive access to the entire Monocle archive, and have priority access to selected product collaborations at *monocle.com*.

03
Never miss an issue
Subscription copies are delivered to your door no matter where you are in the world, and we offer an auto-renewal service to ensure that you never miss an issue.

04
And there's more...
Subscribers benefit from a 10 per cent discount at all Monocle shops, including online, and receive exclusive offers and invitations to events around the world.

Choose your package

Premium one year
12 × issues
+ Porter Sub Club bag

One year
12 × issues
+ Monocle Voyage tote bag

Six months
6 × issues

Chief photographer
Jan Søndergaard

Still life
David Sykes

Images
Alamy
Iwan Baan
Claes Bech-Poulsen
Irina Boersma
Lakrids by Johan Bülow
Sarah Coghill
Ana Cuba
Kirstine Fryd
Getty Images
Studio Oliver Gustav
Mikkel Heriba
Kim Høltermand
Huset-KBH
Per-Anders Jorgensen
Martin Kaufmann
Stamers Kontor
Marie Louise Munkegaard
Freya McOmish
Neel Munthe Brun
Jon Nordstrøm
Rasmus Palsgård
Alastair Philip Wiper
Kasper Ponker
Signe Roderik
Johan Rosenmunthe
Diana Sigfusson
Anders Sune Berg
Chris Tonnesen
Ben Brahem Ziryab

Illustrators
Satoshi Hashimoto
Ceylan Sahin
Tokuma

Writers
Mikaela Aitken
Chloë Ashby
Kristian Baumann
Michael Booth
Melkon Charchoglyan
Mikael Colville-Andersen
Flemming Emil Hansen
Jan Gehl
Nana Hagel
Pete Kempshall
Edward Lawrenson
Sean McGeady
Kay Xander Mellish
Charlie Monaghan
Jeppe Mühlhausen
Jeni Porter
Amy Richardson
Chiara Rimella
Lise Ulrich
Sonia Zhuravlyova

Monocle
EDITOR IN CHIEF AND CHAIRMAN
Tyler Brûlé
EDITOR
Andrew Tuck
CREATIVE DIRECTOR
Richard Spencer Powell

CHAPTER EDITING

Need to know
Amy Richardson

Hotels
Amy Richardson

Food and drink
Michael Booth

Retail
Mikaela Aitken

Things we'd buy
Joe Pickard
Mikaela Aitken

Essays
Amy Richardson

Culture
Chloë Ashby

Design and architecture
Amy Richardson

Sport and fitness
Amy Richardson
Mikaela Aitken

Walks
Amy Richardson
Mikaela Aitken

Resources
Amy Richardson

**The Monocle Travel Guide
Series: Copenhagen**
GUIDE EDITOR
Amy Richardson
ASSOCIATE GUIDE EDITOR
Mikaela Aitken
PHOTO EDITOR
Faye Sakura Rentoule

**The Monocle Travel Guide
Series**
SERIES EDITOR
Joe Pickard
ASSOCIATE EDITOR, BOOKS
Amy Richardson
RESEARCHER/WRITER
Mikaela Aitken
DESIGNER
Sam Brogan
PHOTO EDITORS
Matthew Beaman
Faye Sakura Rentoule
Shin Miura

PRODUCTION
Jacqueline Deacon
Dan Poole
Chloë Ashby
Sean McGeady
Sonia Zhuravlyova

Research
Mikaela Aitken
Melkon Charchoglyan
Charlie Monaghan
Clarissa Pharr
Aliz Tennant
Samantha van Egmond
Ilse Viveros
Kerala Woods
Zayana Zulkiflee

Special thanks
Kathy Ball
Paul Fairclough
Edward Lawrenson

New

The collection

We hope you have found the Monocle Travel Guide to Copenhagen useful, inspiring and entertaining. We're confident it will help you get the most out of your visit to Denmark. There's plenty more to get your teeth into: we have a global suite of guides with many more set to be released in coming months. Cities are fun. Let's explore.

Buy today at all good bookshops
─────
Or you can visit the online stores at: *monocle.com/shop* and *shop.gestalten.com.*

❶ London
The sights, sounds and style

❷ New York
Get a taste for the Big Apple's best

❸ Tokyo
The enigmatic glory of Japan's capital

❹ Hong Kong
Down to business in this vibrant city

❺ Madrid
Captivating capital abuzz with spirit

❻ Bangkok
Stimulate your senses with the exotic

❼ Istanbul
Thrilling fusion of Asia and Europe

❽ Miami
Unpack the Magic City's box of tricks

❾ Rio de Janeiro
Beaches, bars and bossa nova

❿ Paris
Be romanced by the City of Light

⓫ Singapore
Where modernity meets tradition

⓬ Vienna
Waltz through the Austrian capital

⓭ Sydney
Sun, surf and urban delights

⓮ Honolulu
Embrace Hawaii's aloha spirit

⓯ Copenhagen
Cycle through the Danish capital